EVERYONE WAS SILENT

Diane Tarantini

Everyone Was Silent: A Memoir copyright 2024 by Diane Tarantini

All rights reserved. No part of this book may be used or reproduced in any manner whatsoever without written permission from the author.

First edition published by Heard Communications, LLC

Printed in the United States of America

ISBN: 979-8-9853375-3-2

Grateful acknowledgment is made for permission to include an excerpt from "Night Train to Memphis" by Richard Tillinghast, first published in the *Birmingham Poetry Review*.

THE HOLY BIBLE, NEW INTERNATIONAL VERSION®, NIV® Copyright © 1973, 1978, 1984, 2011 by Biblica, Inc.® Used by permission. All rights reserved worldwide.

Edited by Joy Hoppenot

Cover design by Don Patton, Don Patton Creative

Every trip home
is a pilgrimage into the self.
What other way is there
to find out who you are?
I need to follow my footsteps backwards,
bewildered and astonished
into my childhood—
so I can enter the sanctuary of becoming.

From "Night Train to Memphis"
Richard Tillinghast

DEDICATION

To my husband, for your support through all the chaos.
To my children, for your patience while I learned to mother.
To the 42 million survivors of child sexual abuse living in the United States today. I'm sorry for your loss.
And to my community of fellow sibling sexual abuse survivors. I esteem you greatly.

PREFACE

Ever since the fourth grade I've known two things. I'd get counseling and I'd write a book. Both for the same reason: a challenging childhood.

Even at nine years old, I knew someday I'd need professional help sorting through the various events I experienced. As for writing a book, I always believed my story compelling and that what I went through—the choices I made, the problems I solved—would help others in a similar situation, and possibly their loved ones too.

In the back of the book are a number of resources I've collected over the years—books and websites I've found valuable. I hope they'll help you find your way also.

Now, friend, let's go over a few things before you proceed.

- All the names in this story have been changed for the privacy of everyone concerned.
- Everything you're about to read is true. However, the character of Eve is a composite of a number of my female friends.

- In this story, there will be times I speak of child sexual abuse, and there are scenes portraying physical violence. If either topic makes you anxious or uncomfortable, skipping over those scenes might be best for you.

EVERYONE WAS SILENT

Diane Tarantini

PROLOGUE

I REMEMBER.

In the first home my husband Chad and I owned.

The year was 1993.

Our firstborn child would soon turn two.

I'd just lifted her from the bath and patted her dry.

Still in her hooded towel, she flitted around the bathroom on her tiptoes performing what we called her "Da Doo Doo Dance," named after the silly song she sang during this ritual.

All damp velvety innocence in the steam-filled bathroom.

My stare became a squint, then a grimace as a thought came suddenly to mind,

A knowing.

This is what I looked like when it began.

My body boasted no curves: no breasts, no hips.

No hair anywhere other than on my head.

I was only a little girl ...

When my older brother began sneaking into my room at night.

PART ONE

The Healing
1995–2002

CHAPTER ONE
The D-Word

"So tell me, why are you here today?" my doctor asked.

I tugged the hem of the exam gown over my knees. If I answered truthfully, everything would change. Like it does when a child is born or a loved one dies.

"I yell at my kids, our two little girls, a lot."

"How's your sleep, and your sex life? Have you gained or lost weight recently?"

"Fine. Okay. I still have some baby weight."

He asked me to describe the overall quality of my life, to rank it on a scale of one to ten.

I'm pissed off most of the time, which is why I made this appointment, I thought. What normal person kicks their beagle? Plus, I feel like a mummy, all wrapped up, life muffled. I don't smell or taste much anymore, don't feel excitement or joy. Only frequent anger and the need to conceal it.

"I don't know, a four, maybe? I used to be happy all the time with super-high energy." As I sighed, my lips flapped.

Dr. Davis rolled his stool toward me. "Sounds like moderate depression. Does anyone in your family have a depression diagnosis?"

The small white room closed in. "My mother does."

While he bent to write, I wondered if he heard me. He held out a prescription, his fingers warm against mine. "Be on the lookout for side effects. And come back to see me in a month."

That afternoon in my car outside Walmart, I stared at the prescription in my lap. I folded it twice, opened it back up, and smoothed it flat against my thigh. If I fill this prescription, does it mean I'm crazy? Is this the first step to becoming Mom? I wiped perspiration from my upper lip. That was how my brothers tormented me, saying I'd end up exactly like her, which meant nuts or fat or both.

After I filled the prescription, I sat in the car and polished off a dozen bite-sized peanut butter cups. It's just one pill a day. That's not so bad. If it makes me nice to the girls and Lacy again, I should do it, right?

Within a month, I felt like my old self. Sort of. I called my medicine my "duck drug," explained to my husband Chad how it made everything—good or bad—roll off my back. I had dry mouth and my hands shook, but I didn't yell anymore. As Chad hugged me, he said he was glad I was happy again.

Happy? I'm not sure I'd go that far.

I'd started feeling unsettled again a few years earlier, during a phone call with my mother. I'd been making Sophia's lunch when the phone rang.

"Why did you name Sophia after Chad's mother? Do you like her better?"

Typical call from Mom. No hello. She just plunged right in. I reminded Mom that Sophia had her middle name. And besides, we had named our daughter almost four years ago. Recalling Chad's recent suggestion, I tried to sound as if I valued what she had to say.

"Why don't you try arguing with her less?" he'd said. "She says black. You say white. She says good. You say bad. Why don't you tell her you'll think about it and get back to her?" It worked really well, when I remembered to do it. So did changing the subject.

I asked Mom how many doctor appointments she and Dad had that week.

"That's not why I called." She'd phoned to tell me that Jude, one of my three older brothers, was coming to visit. First he'd stay with her and Dad, then Mimi and Aunt Peg. He'd visit Chad and me, too, maybe for a week.

I grabbed the edge of the kitchen table when my knees went soft. I told Mom I had to go, then pressed the off button. The phone clattered on the glass tabletop.

Sophia touched my arm. "What's wrong, Mommy? Your face went all funny. Are you going to throw up?"

My head felt like it was up near the ceiling looking down. At the counter, I picked up my plate and returned to the table. "You were playing with the dog, Soph. Did you wash your hands? Go wash your hands."

I opened the refrigerator and stared inside. He can't visit. I won't let him.

After I put Sophia down for her nap, I found myself wishing we'd never moved back to West Virginia. Determined to leave the mountain state behind, I moved to Washington, D.C. after college. A year later, Chad followed me and we enjoyed big city life for three years.

Concerned about D.C.'s escalating crime rate, we decided to relocate to a smaller city, a safer one. We closed our eyes, poked our fingers at a map, and that's where we ended up—Cincinnati. I worked downtown in a fancy brownstone. Chad commuted thirty minutes to his job with an insurance office in the suburbs.

Sophia was born in Cincinnati, and despite my past desire to remain child-free, I immediately fell in love with her dark curls and full cherry mouth.

A couple of years later at the local mall, Chad stunned me by saying, "I want to move back to West Virginia."

As we stood beside the sand pit where Sophia was filling up and spilling out her pastel pink Stride Rite shoes, I threw a quiet fit. With sob-squinty eyes, I faced him. "Don't you remember me saying I'm a big city girl?"

Chad thought hard before answering. "If you hate it after a year, we'll move someplace else." Knowing Chad always kept his promises, I agreed.

And really, for the most part, I'd loved being back home. The lower crime rate and cost of living, the manageable traffic. But there was a downside. The return to West Virginia meant living much closer to my parents, which meant that when Jude visited them, he would be closer to me, a fact that made me very uncomfortable.

Twenty times that night in our third-floor bedroom, I flipped my pillow to the cool side. It was after midnight when I sat up. I knew what to do. I slipped on my robe and crept downstairs. At the dining room table, I fed paper into my old school typewriter. I typed *dear*, then yanked the sheet from the roller, inserted another page, and began again.

> *Jude:*
> *I hear through the grapevine that you are in West Virginia. Hopefully you will have a nice visit with Mom and Dad. Hopefully, you will not wear out your welcome as you have in the past. You must have been blind and/or ignorant not to have seen the incredible stress and pain your overlong visits caused them. Please do as they ask and only stay two weeks or less. I would really hate to again see them as incredibly angry and upset as they have been after your last visits.*
>
> *As for myself, I am asking you not to call or visit me and my family. I am very angry and nervous around you for past*

and present reasons. I hope I can work through this someday. However, that probably won't be until I can afford therapy. Frankly, I think you could use a ~~little~~ lot of therapy yourself.

Tonight I racked my brain for excuses and lies to avoid seeing you, but in the end, I decided honesty is the best policy. I do not want to make myself sick by agreeing to see or talk to you. Please do not try.

There you have it.
Dina

In the morning I sent the letter via certified mail.

Mom called three days later demanding to know what it said.

"None of your business."

"What did you say to him? He's devastated."

"Boo-hoo," I mouthed. When Mom said Jude had canceled his visit, I smiled.

CHAPTER TWO
Baby Boy

TWO YEARS LATER, DURING A WEEKEND AT SEAWORLD IN OHIO, A pressing desire surprised me. I wanted a third child. In college, I was sure I didn't want children. But then I fell in love with Chad and he wanted several. Six, to be exact. To my relief, he agreed when I told him I'd birth one baby. For him. If I had to.

By the time Sophia turned three, I adored her and parenting. "Maybe we should have another, so Sophia won't be an only child," I suggested. That night Chad had scootched closer to me on the love seat and told me he was happy to oblige. Eventually Lark came along.

That day at SeaWorld, offspring of all kinds surrounded us. Human babies, dolphin babies, whale babies. Infants in strollers and backpacks and slings, toddlers taking their first zombie-like steps. Beneath the marine smell I recognized one of my favorite scents—clean baby.

On Sunday afternoon, during the whale show, I leaned over and whispered in Chad's ear. "Want to have another baby? We could try for a boy."

He faced me, radiant. "Really? Yes! Boy or girl, I don't care. Let's go for it."

As Shamu smacked her tail against the water, I chuckled and gave him a peck on the cheek.

Hoping to make a boy child, I visited the library for a how-to-determine-your-baby's-gender book. I followed the author's directions carefully—check this, chart that. Even so, my cycle came and went each month. What were we doing wrong? A friend suggested we try an ovulation kit. Success!

Eighteen weeks into the pregnancy, at the ultrasound clinic, the radiologist briskly rubbed his hands together and said, "This being West Virginia and all, I don't want to start a family feud, so do you or don't you want to know the gender of your child?"

I clapped and said yes. Chad glared and said no. When I pooched out my lower lip, he crossed his arms and refused to smile no matter how many times I batted my eyelashes.

"I like surprises. My family does too."

I laced my fingers beneath my chin. "How about we find out but don't tell anyone?"

Chad sighed and nodded.

Wheeling his stool to face the screen, the doctor pointed with his pen and spoke more to Chad than me. "See that right there? That's what makes your little guy a guy."

On the exam table, I squealed. The doctor gave Chad a little shove and asked if he was okay. Chad's face was so close to the ultrasound screen his breath left fog.

"It's really a boy?" he asked.

As I watched him, I felt as if I was connected to a bike pump with little puffs of air swelling my heart.

Since I'd delivered one baby with an epidural and one without —which feels, by the way, like you're pushing out a globe—for my third and final birth, I wanted drugs. In fact, at one of my prenatal appointments, I suggested to Dr. Davis that he write in my file, preferably in all caps, "Patient wants drugs as soon as she enters the hospital." I think he forgot.

I remember my labor and delivery nurse hurrying to answer a knock at the door and how I strained to comprehend the whispers out in the hall. Back at my bedside, the nurse picked up my hand and stroked my fingers one by one. My eyes narrowed.

"Sweetheart, I just got word that the anesthesiologist is tending to a more emergent case."

I struggled to sit up. "What is more emergent than a baby exiting my body through an opening the size of my palm?"

She told me she'd be right back, and two minutes later she returned, a syringe nestled in her hand. "Would you like some Nubain, honey? It'll calm you down, take the edge off your pain."

My bottom lip quivered as a splitting sensation began deep within me, forcing my pelvic bones in opposite directions. I blinked hard and nodded.

When the Nubain entered my bloodstream, contentment sped through me, bathing my nerves and coaxing them toward almost tranquility. I felt a smile land on my face, like I was Mrs. Potato Head and someone had just stuck red smiley lips beneath my nose.

I stretched out my arm toward her. "That's really nice. I like it a lot. Some more, please?"

She smirked as she checked my pulse. "Sorry, no."

Unlike most mothers I know, I wasn't in a hurry to return home after delivering a baby. Home is where the work is. I enjoyed every one of the forty-eight hours following the birth of each of my children. People fed me. They changed the baby's diaper. If I shivered they brought me blankets. All I had to do was eat, sleep, and snuggle my precious. And listen to the nurses' contradictory lactation advice: On demand. On schedule. Breastfeeding should hurt. It should not.

On the morning we were to be discharged, I lay in the hospital bed and marveled at Wyatt asleep in my arms. He looked exactly like Chad—creamy skin, dark eyes, full red lips. A shiny happiness spread through me, almost like Nubain. With a boy child, our family was complete.

Wyatt suffered from colic. Kind of. He didn't have it continuously—only from five to six each evening—the "witching hour." As he wailed, the girls begged me to make him stop. Or they complained of boredom. What could they do now? Lacy would be underfoot, whining for supper, when Chad came through the front door, arms open, lips puckered. I'd turn away as everything inside of me constricted, then I'd order it all to release so I could face him with a carefully applied cheerful mommy expression.

During the next few months, two things helped me tolerate the witching hour. One was the vacuum cleaner. Vacuum off—screaming baby. Vacuum on—cooing infant. The trick worked beautifully for Wyatt, but did nothing for me. What helped me was alcohol.

When we began trying to conceive Wyatt, I threw away my antidepressant meds. Dr. Davis assured me I didn't need to, said the drug posed no threat to the baby, but I wanted to be as safe as possible. Now that my little guy was here, I thought I wouldn't need my duck drug again. Wrong.

At the end of each day my forehead pounded and angry words collected in my mouth, ready. But if I drank a beer or a glass of wine, a physiological whoosh of relief would course through me—a tide of serenity. It felt familiar. It felt like Nubain. Oh, that's nice. Some more, please? Sorry, no. You're breastfeeding an infant. The subtle numbing of all things negative and slight augmenting of all things positive were comforting, but I knew better than to depend on the alcohol too much.

CHAPTER THREE
Reckoning Time

A FEW MONTHS LATER WHEN THE FREQUENT URGE TO KICK LACY resumed, I knew Mean Mommy was back, so I returned to Dr. Davis. In the exam room, he paused his note-taking.

"Is there something else I should know, something I'm missing?" he asked. I didn't look up from my fuchsia pedicure. "Antidepressants are often only a Band-Aid for a deeper problem. Is there a deeper problem?"

I liked Dr. Davis. And I trusted him. But telling my secret felt scarier than keeping it a while longer. Then it occurred to me that though I hadn't peeped in thirty years, my predicament hadn't gone away.

"Growing up, I was abused. Sexually."

Part of me wanted to raise my eyes and see what someone looked like when they heard my secret. Instead, I kept my chin to my chest. If I saw his face, what would I see? Shock, pity, revulsion? I picked at my exam gown and wished I could take back my confession.

Tick. Tock. Tick. Tock. Finally, I glanced up and discovered the reason Dr. Davis became a physician—compassion. His eyes were twin seas of kindness. My worries receded.

After Dr. Davis handed me my prescription, he tore off another page and flipped it to the blank side. "I'm writing down a few resources, a couple of people you can talk to. If you don't deal with this, things might get worse. Does Chad know?" I said yes, but that wasn't entirely true.

As we left the exam room, Dr. Davis rested his hand on my shoulder. "Come back in six months, but call sooner if you need anything. Promise?"

At home, I phoned my friend Eve to tell her about my appointment and give her a quick overview of my problematic childhood.

"Please tell me you're kidding. Never mind. I know you're not. What a creep! And your parents didn't—"

I told her I was considering counseling like Dr. Davis suggested.

"Good. Great. You've got to. For your marriage, for your kids. For you!"

Before we hung up, she pressed me to talk to Chad that night. I assured her I would, but I didn't.

Instead, after supper as I loaded the dishwasher, I made excuses. Therapy is too expensive. And too hard. Maybe I'd do it when the kids got older.

A month later, Chad climbed to the third floor where I was reading to Sophia and Lark on our bed. Wyatt was already down for the night. In his fist, Chad clutched some papers. The pages trembled.

"Soph, take Lark downstairs so I can talk to Mommy alone, please." His tone was stern and Sophia's bottom lip quivered. Lark whimpered. One by one, Chad scooped up the girls and set them near the steps. "We'll be down soon to get you all ready for bed."

What did Chad want to discuss? He was watching the girls go down the stairs so I couldn't tell if he was mad or sad. When he turned to face me, he held out the papers.

"What is this?"

I took the crumpled pages and skimmed the words. It was a short story I wrote a few years back. About a woman who duct-taped a man to a chair while explaining her reason for killing him—because of all the terrible things he'd done to her. She clicked off the safety on her gun and pointed it at his crotch. He pinched his knees together and between gasps begged her not to shoot, not to shoot him there. The woman squinted her right eye and aimed at his zipper. She said goodbye and squeezed the trigger. As he took his final blubbering breath, her satisfied smile was the last thing he saw.

"Is she you, and I'm him?" Chad asked.

"Of course not! It's about Jude, not you."

Chad's breath was a tire leaking air. He didn't say anything for a minute, but pinned me with his eyes. "You need help."

The preschool where Eve and I enrolled our kids wasn't a drop-off program. After the children were situated in their classrooms, the parents, mostly moms, gathered in the building's basement. Usually we hosted guest speakers, but sometimes we chatted about parenting issues or where to go out to eat.

About a week after Chad confronted me, the preschool parent discussion turned to sexual abuse. Nearly every woman shared an experience. Not me. As I listened closely to the stories and ached for each woman, I realized for the first time how childhood sexual abuse was far more prevalent than I ever suspected.

One woman described the time her grandfather abused her. Only one time? I thought. You're so lucky. Another woman told how her foster brother messed with her a couple of times, but when she started sleeping in her clothes, he left her alone. I grimaced. Why didn't I think of that?

"Both of my brothers abused me," said a lovely blonde, her voice soft. Eve nudged me. I asked the woman if she still spoke to her siblings. She nodded. "And after I went through counseling, I even forgave them."

One of the other mothers snorted and said if that was her, she'd never talk to her brothers again. In fact, she'd "sue their sick butts."

As I drove the kids home that day, I considered the blonde with the bad brothers. She forgave them? Therapy can do that? After lunch, when the girls and Wyatt went down for their naps, I found her number in the phone book and dialed it.

"That situation with your brothers … Where did you, or do you, go for counseling? How hard is it? Do you cry every time?"

"Oh, Dina, you too? I'm so sorry. Do I cry every time? Pretty much, and I threw up once, but you've got to do it. Honestly, it's the hardest thing ever, but it's also the best."

After we put the kids to bed that night, I asked Chad if we could talk. On the living room sofa, I told him about my conversation with the gal from preschool. He squeezed my hands. "Please say you'll do it."

"But I'm scared."

"I am too, but I want you to get better. I don't know your whole story, but what I do know is you need help for whatever happened. Call that place tomorrow. Please?"

I nodded. He was right. I always knew I'd get counseling someday. As difficult as I knew it would be, now that I'd committed, I couldn't wait to start, couldn't wait for the whole thing to be over and behind me. I was done telling myself I didn't have the time, the money, or the guts.

CHAPTER FOUR
The Truth

My counselor Jamie reminded me of a school girl with her dark curls, playground-ruddy cheeks, and eager smile. As we settled into facing chairs, she told me she usually worked with kids, but the clinic paired her with me due to my childhood issues. "Why don't you tell me your story so we can decide if we're a good fit? And if it's easier, when you're talking, call yourself 'Little Dina.'" She picked up her pen and nodded. "When you're ready."

Though I'd waited all my life for a chance to tell my story, my heart now thudded in my chest. I felt both free and freaked out. Hugging my ribs, I pictured my childhood home, a brick box with white and brown striped awnings, set behind a large maple tree. From the street, our house appeared small and innocuous except for the six-foot-high stone wall along the driveway. My mother became anxious when any of us stood near the wall, especially me—the youngest child, the only girl.

All three of my brothers loved to hurl themselves off the wall to the cement driveway below. Afraid of heights, I'd stand a few feet from the edge and cheer them on until Mom appeared in the dining room window, waving and calling warnings. As high as it was, the wall wasn't what I feared. I feared the house. The house goaded

Jude into action, and after the first time, it persuaded him he could do it again and again.

Often as I lay waiting in my bed, I formulated plans. Hide our calico cat Ginger under the covers and beg her to spring out and claw his face. Wrap myself tightly with the sheet like a TV dinner enchilada. On the nights when my door inched open, I clenched my mind and body and hoped to God that fear, like a pheromone, wouldn't leak out. But it always did, cold as a melting popsicle.

Jamie repeated her invitation to speak and I realized I hadn't said anything. I told her how my childhood bedroom was barely pink, a teaspoon of blood in a bucket of cream. My twin bed frame and dresser were French Provincial—ivory with gold trim. Here and there, smears of cherry-colored lip gloss and nail polish marred the surfaces.

One summer Mom suggested we redecorate my room. Dad and I picked out an unfinished furniture set: a chest of drawers, a corner desk with a peg leg, and a set of shelves. He stained each section a honey color and assembled the unit himself.

Because I was wild about horses, all four walls were plastered with horse and pony posters. Equine models of all sizes, as well as miniature saddles and bridles, filled my shelves. Most of all, I treasured my gleaming copper model of a quarter horse. He was so heavy, more than once I told myself he'd make a good weapon.

Not long after my bedroom makeover, when my parents ordered wall-to-wall carpet for the first floor of the house, Mom let me select what I wanted in my bedroom. She winced when I chose shag carpeting the color of green M&Ms. Still, she honored my request. For a week I adored her for letting me have pasture-colored carpet, then I went back to my eye-rolling teenager ways.

My hamster Houdini's cage sat on the floor beside my bed. If I wasn't diligent about cleaning it, the sharp ammonia scent of his urine made my eyes water. Like his namesake, he was an escape artist. In the middle of the night he often finagled his way out of his fancy trilevel habitat, but he always returned the next morning. I longed for similar powers.

From my bedroom window, I could survey the backyard. In summer, Mom's cutting gardens erupted in color with rows of zinnias and Shasta daisies, fuzzy purple ageratum, orange and yellow marigolds, and snapdragons with tiny puckered mouths. Every year, spring until frost, I kept two to five vases of cut flowers in my room. Mom insisted that was too many. She didn't grok—to understand profoundly and intuitively (Gosh, I loved that word!)—that I had to bring the outside in because I couldn't take the inside out.

Long ago, Dad had rigged my doorknob with wire so I could never lock anyone out. "It's safer this way, Honey Pot. You can't lock your mom out every time she ticks you off. What if the house catches fire with you locked inside here?"

Jamie listened without interrupting as I described my childhood. From time to time she handed me tissues, and whenever I stalled, she encouraged me with her eyes. At last my words petered out. My secret was known. I peeked up from my lap and noticed her eyes were wet too. To keep from smiling, I nibbled the inside of my mouth. I wasn't sure why her tears made me happy.

Jamie leaned forward and held out her hands, but I didn't take them. "First, let me say how very sorry I am that all of this happened. It was very wrong of your brother, and your parents let you down big time, didn't they?"

I sniffed as I nodded. Someone besides me got it. I waited for her to ask the question I dreaded: "Why didn't you say something, tell somebody?" But she didn't.

She surrounded my hands with hers. "This was not your fault. You know that, right?"

I didn't answer.

"I'm serious. You are not to blame for what happened. Got that? Whatever you did, you did to survive."

"I suck my thumb! I still suck my thumb." My face crumpled, and the tears began again.

Jamie held out the box of tissues. "I wish I could rewrite your childhood in order to give you a shiny safe one with no bad stuff." She sighed and shook her head. "But I can't, so here's what I think we should do."

At Jamie's urging, I booked ninety-minute sessions instead of sixty, in hopes I'd get better faster. As a result, the funds in our bank account dwindled rapidly. Each time I updated the register in our little savings account booklet, I cringed. What if we experienced a financial crisis? After discussing the concern with Jamie and Chad, I decided to tell my parents about my counseling and request their help.

This would be the third time I would tell them about the abuse.

The first time, I was sixteen and Jude was away at college. I had enjoyed two blissful years without his nocturnal visits to my room. But due to his penchant for drugs and alcohol, Jude ended up leaving college. With him returning home, I feared the abuse would resume, so I made myself tell my parents.

Dad was watching the news with a World War II history book open on his lap. Mom was reading a paperback, a lit cigarette and a glass of Tab diet cola on the table beside her. I stood in front of the television.

Dad peered over his thick-framed reading glasses. "What is it, Honey Pot?"

When I asked if I could speak with him and Mom, he closed his book and motioned to the rust-colored recliner across from him. I turned off the TV and sat.

"Jude comes into my room at night."

I dug at the hardened warts that framed each of my fingernails.

Why weren't my parents responding? I looked up—first at Dad, then Mom. Their eyes were squinted, their heads tilted.

I raised my voice, as if they were hard of hearing. "Jude comes into my room at night." I couldn't think of another way to make them understand what I was saying. Even if I could, I was fairly confident nothing else would come out of my mouth because my lips felt superglued together and my tongue like a chalkboard eraser.

Come on, Dad, I hissed inside my head. You've got multiple degrees, two in psychology, one from Harvard. Surely you can grok this.

At last he spoke. "We'll take care of it."

I thought Dad understood what I was saying, but he didn't. He was super smart, but clearly, he did not know everything.

Mom didn't get it, either. Years later, she admitted she and Dad thought Jude was sneaking into my bedroom to watch me sleep.

You've got to be kidding. I wanted to yell, "What kind of mother thinks when a guy creeps into a girl's bedroom in the middle of the night, it's to watch her sleep?" If I was a mom, I'd know. I'd stop it. Right then I decided if I ever had kids, I'd hang giant sleigh bells on all their bedroom doors.

A week before Jude's homecoming, Mom tapped on my bedroom door and entered with a box heaped high with every pot, pan, and skillet she owned.

"Stack these behind your door every night." She spoke in a whisper, as if Jude was already back, like she was afraid of him too. "If anyone tries to get in your room, we'll hear."

I moved toward her, thinking, this is the best they can do? I placed my hands on either side of the box, careful not to touch hers. "What about when you fix supper? Won't you need them?"

"I'll come get them. And at bedtime I'll bring them back."

I wanted to tell her it was a stupid plan, a cowardly one. Instead,

I merely slammed the door shut and gave it, and everyone on the other side, the middle finger.

Feeble as the plan was, it worked. After Jude moved back home, he never again stepped inside my pale pink bedroom. Still, whenever he was in the house, I felt his inappropriate energy, the way it vibrated the air like a plucked guitar string. I did my best to avoid his eyes, sure that in his smirk I'd recognize a boast of what I'd been to him.

Each night at dinner, whenever Jude asked me to pass something—the mixed vegetables, the pitcher of milk—as I reached across the table, I focused on his copper-colored curls and imagined him being what a big brother should be: a hero, not a villain. Not a traitor.

I also told my parents about the abuse when I was pregnant with Lark. Chad, Sophia, and I had recently moved from an apartment to a three-story brick home. We'd only lived there a week when Mom called. Sophia was down for her nap and I was washing the kitchen walls—thinking how I wanted Chad to paint the cabinets white so the room would be lighter and brighter—and the phone rang.

"What was in that letter?"

It took me a minute to figure out what Mom was huffing about, then I remembered the certified letter I'd sent to Jude two years ago telling him to never visit again. I tried to change the subject but Mom would not drop it.

"Why don't you talk to him? Why won't you see him? You used to."

"You want to know why I won't talk to Jude?" I hissed. "He only took away my whole childhood! Coming into my room practically every night to paw and pant and use me as his fucking personal bowling ball." I continued with my expletive-filled diatribe until I was hoarse. Then I dropped the phone into its base without saying goodbye. As I climbed the stairs, the phone rang. It kept ringing. I kept climbing.

The next day, Mom phoned again. "Your father's on the other line. Tell him what you told me yesterday, all of it. Why you won't talk to Jude."

My parents had obviously planned their strategy, and to their credit, it worked.

"Get it out. Get it off your chest," my mother coached. Her years of therapy paid off that day. The psychobabble I despised fairly gushed through the phone.

"Dina," Mom said, "exactly what happened all those nights? What did he do to you?"

Sophia was at a playdate, but Chad was home for lunch. The conversation with my parents started out calm, but like the day before, it quickly flamed out of control. As my voice rose, Chad came running.

"Excuse me? Were you not listening when I assaulted your ears yesterday? Do you not remember me asking you to tell him to leave me alone when I was however old I was? Do you know how lucky you are I don't hate you? You didn't protect me for all those years, and when I finally asked you to, you gave me pans. Fucking pots and pans!"

"Did it ever happen again?" my father asked quietly.

"Did what?"

"Did it ever happen again?" Dad repeated.

Even though he couldn't see me, I shook my head. "No," I responded softly.

"That's because I told him I'd kick the shit out of him if he ever came near you again."

Across the kitchen, Chad leaned against the dishwasher. His forehead creased and his hands fisted, but he didn't move or speak. Because this was his chance to hear more about my childhood.

My parents stayed silent, so I spoke again. "Still, it's going to take years and thousands of dollars to fix me, you know. All because you never did anything. Not only that, Jude did stuff to other people too. He ..." I hesitated to go on.

Chad came and stood next to me, so I moved over by the sink. When he followed, I twisted to face him, furious. He retreated with his hands up, his eyes wounded.

Mom started up again. "You should have—"

"What did you want me to say, Mom? That my holes were his? I was just a little girl and I knew it was wrong. He's five years older. Why didn't he?"

Chad took the phone from me. "Enough," he growled into the receiver before he hung up. Minutes later, in his arms, I finally stopped shaking. He led me into the living room, covered me with an afghan on the sofa, and stayed until my sobbing hiccups faded.

As he stood to leave, I grabbed his hand and pressed it to my cheek. "I'm sorry."

He nodded, his eyes glistening. "Me too."

The third time I told my parents about the abuse—four years after my second disclosure—I put it in writing.

Dear Mom and Dad:

I have two favors I must ask of you. I don't want to ask them but I must. I wanted to do this alone but I cannot.

The sexual abuse that I suffered at the hands of Jude during my childhood is taking its toll on my happiness, my family life, and my sanity.

I am in therapy. I do not want this to drag on forever. My therapist has suggested longer sessions and the addition of a weekly group session. This will be very draining mentally, physically, and financially.

> *The first favor I need is for you all to babysit one afternoon a week for as long as it takes.*
>
> *The second favor I need is for any financial assistance you could offer. Once a week sessions are expensive. Twice a week is out of the question without help.*
>
> *Finally, if we go forward with this, please know (a) I will not discuss any of my "trauma work" with you and (b) I will never ever be in contact with Jude again, so do not expect that.*
>
> *Dina*
>
> *P.S. An additional request I have is that you just once say that what Jude did was very wrong. I know it is hard because he is your son but if he wasn't, don't you think you would have reacted differently? I can only hope so.*

Their response arrived within a week. Dad wrote his letter on yellow legal-pad paper and folded it around a check. The amount was enough to cover my counseling and then some. I studied my father's neat handwriting. He'd always admired Thomas Edison and his penmanship. When Dad was a teenager, he located a sample of Edison's handwriting and copied it over and over until his writing was identical.

> *Dear Dina:*
>
> *I am rushing to get some cash to you. Enclosed is a check. I will free up more cash pretty soon. Go ahead with therapy. Do you know people who can vouch for the credentials of the therapist? If you can, get me the details of what the therapist proposes.*
>
> *Mother and I are both convinced that Jude is a sorry SOB and I am convinced that he is a very evil member of our family. He gets no sympathy from me and very little money, be assured of that. I don't want him around here and he knows that much.*

We will do whatever you want us to do. We are so sorry for all this mess has presented you with.

Try to be your cheerful and good-natured self, the person we are always proud of. We love you dearly. We are looking forward to looking after your little ones.

We just cannot understand how Jude got so poisoned against you three and how much we did not suspect what was going on behind our backs.

If you wish, I will give you money to pay your bills. Keep track of your medical expenses for the IRS. I will be in touch with you. Let me know your needs.

Love from us always,
Mom and Dad
P.S. We will never excuse what he did to you.

Smiling, I read Dad's harsh words regarding Jude several times. I was glad he didn't give Jude money, thrilled he didn't want him around. I wanted everyone on my side. But Dad's plea for me to stay good-natured made me bristle. Was he telling me to be quiet? Was his check hush money? Another line in his letter annoyed me: "how much we did not suspect what was going on behind our backs." Great point, Dad. Over the years I'd wondered that very thing so many times.

How did Mom not catch Jude? She hardly ever slept at night. Plus, our bedrooms were right beside each other. The only thing in between was the medicine closet, a two-foot-wide storage space where Mom stowed her Bufferin, Rolaids, and several prescription medications, along with Band-Aids, Merthiolate, and the orange-flavored St. Joseph chewable aspirin my brothers and I munched like candy. Did she seriously not hear the creaking of my door whenever Jude nudged it open?

It was as if my mother's internal clock was broken, the way she

27

napped during the day and roamed the house at night. Since I was a light sleeper, her activity usually woke me. Some nights she left her bedroom in search of something to eat. Others she sat in the living room smoking cigarettes and drinking Tab.

Frequently she demanded that Dad keep her company in the middle of the night. "You never talk to me. You don't help around the house. I feel so alone." She recited the list of his shortcomings top to bottom and side to side. "Tell me how you feel, Paul. I'm not a mind reader."

Often I cranked the volume on my clock radio as loud as it would go and wrapped my pillow around my head like a giant pair of earmuffs. Say something, Dad. Be a man. Fight back. Sometimes I wished he'd hit her to shut her up. I chanted, *Divorce her!* over and over in my mind. I fantasized about life with a normal mom who wasn't overweight and sick all the time. A mom who wasn't a whiny chain-smoker.

I hardly blamed Dad for not rescuing me. The only time he woke from his snoring sleep was when Mom forced him.

I stared at Dad's letter, certain I knew what he thought as he read my note. He probably wondered why I didn't scream, "Stop!" or "Get out of my room, you pervert!"

At first, silence was my strategy with Jude. If I didn't say yes, if I didn't say anything, wasn't that the same thing as saying no? It wasn't until years later when I saw a billboard declaring, "Silence is compliance" that I learned silence is sometimes construed as permission.

In time, silence became my cell within the prison of my family. If I didn't protest, didn't say a word the first, second, or third time, what sense did it make for me to object on the tenth or twentieth time? I believed I had relinquished my right of refusal. Somewhere during my adolescence, a statute of limitations had expired.

For years I condemned my parents' lack of response, but not my own. Didn't I have excuses, multiple and legitimate, for my shut mouth? For starters, it was as if I was allergic to telling the truth about Jude. Every time I tried, my lips seemed to double in size and become clumsy. My throat mimicked anaphylactic shock—swelling, closing. *I can't breathe. I'm going to die!*

The thought of accusing Jude was already terrifying, but what of the aftermath, the consequences? As a teenager, I made a list of the pros and cons of speaking out:

<u>Cons</u>
What if no one believes me?
What if they blame me?
What if in his rage Jude begins to beat me daily like he does our brother Tom?
What if my announcement tears our family apart?
What if the world forever sees me as "that poor girl whose brother … ?"
What if no boy ever wants me because I'm "that poor girl whose brother … ?"
What if our community shuns my family?
What if Dad loses his job over our disgrace?
What if Jude gets sent away?

<u>Pro</u>
He'll stop coming into my room.

With only one pro, telling on Jude hardly seemed worth it. Was I worth it?

Afterward I'd have to stare into Jude's face. My handsomest brother, my most exciting sibling—the one who did wheelies on his motorcycle while I clutched his waist, the one who showed me secret wooded places with rope swings over swollen, rushing creeks, the one I raced with down frozen hills, crowded on a Flexible Flyer sled. The one who did this to me.

I loathed what he did to me. It disgusted me that he must have known it was wrong, yet he did it anyway. But I didn't hate him. I wanted him to stop, but I didn't want him to detest me for stopping him, for exposing him.

I was frozen, stuck tight in a family that hurt me by violating me and by failing to protect me. Stuck in a family where everyone was silent.

In grade school I believed aliens placed me in my home. I did not belong to the family I lived with. Surely I belonged in my friend Sherri Wilson's family. They were just like the family in *The Waltons*. Every night at bedtime, they hugged and said goodnight to one another. That was how family was supposed to be. Sometimes I stared into the night sky and whispered, "I want a do-over, aliens. Do you hear me? Take me to the Wilsons."

Jude didn't arrive hungry every night, but he may as well have. Each night, whether the house shifted with an audible noise or not, my body chose not to fight or flee, but to freeze. I never gave up hope that my tightly fused limbs, my fury-red face pressed into my Mary Poppins pillowcase, or my stiff back would deter him.

Nothing I did ever stopped him. Beneath my pink-tulips-in-green-vases quilt, I twined my legs together inside my nightgown and pretended to sleep while he went straight to his work—the leveraging apart of my ankles, knees, and thighs, then the separating and unsticking of the velveteen place between my legs.

I imagined flattening myself so thin I could slip under my window screen and float next door to beg our neighbors, Mr. and Mrs. McCallister, for help. Of all us kids, I believed they loved me best because I visited them every day. Their house was my haven. It drew me to them and held me close, safe. I imagined my flattened ghost self tapping on the window near where Mrs. Mac slept. Wake up. Please. I need you. I'll stick my arm out my window and you stick your arm out yours. Our houses are so close together, maybe we can hold hands.

And inside my head, I yelled for help, shrill and desperate. I thought of the Amazing Kreskin on television. Every week he read people's minds and made stuff levitate. If he could bend spoons with his brain, surely I could wake my parents, or the Macs, or my other two brothers—Mark or Tom—with my silent screams. No one ever heard.

CHAPTER FIVE
Consequences

A WEEK AFTER DAD SENT MONEY, MOM PHONED. "I CALLED JUDE."

On my way up the stairs, I paused, my chest tight. Did she not believe me? I strained to catch what she said next. "I had to hear it from him, that he did it." I didn't speak, didn't breathe. "He said it's true. Oh, Dina …"

Sometimes I pictured Mom with her stiff, quirky nurse's cap bobby pinned into her dark curls, but now I imagined her age-spotted hands trembling as she waited for Jude to answer the phone. How did she work up the nerve to make the call? As a nurse, she could stomach the blood and guts of strangers, but she freaked out whenever my brothers beat each other up. "Call your father," she used to say to me. "Tell him to come home and do something with these boys!"

What must it have been like for my fragile mother to ask my powerful brother, "Did you do what your sister said?"

And Jude didn't call me a liar, didn't attempt to disprove me. His response imbued me with an odd sense of triumph, as if I'd won some sort of medal.

"Why didn't you tell us?" Mom whispered. "Why didn't you scream?"

Everything in me tensed. "Mom, don't even go there. Don't tell me what I should have done. A little child who's being abused can't scream, can't tell. I know that now from therapy."

"Okay, I'm sorry."

"I need you and Dad to help me with something. I'm trying to figure out when it all started. I have this visual memory. My bed is in the middle of the room. There is a six-foot ladder in there and drop cloths all around. There's no carpeting yet. When was that?"

Mom sputtered. "You don't know how old you were? How long this lasted? How often did he do this?"

My fingernails bit into my palms. "Dang it, Mom! It was all the time. Don't you understand? I remember very little of my childhood. Not the good stuff. Not the bad stuff. I have no concept of time. It's all gone."

"Oh my gosh. You poor thing." Mom thought a moment. "The first time we painted your room, you were three."

I began to wail. "No, Mom! Don't let me be three. I don't want it to have gone on that long. That can't be right!" But then I remembered the knowing I experienced. When I witnessed Sophia doing her da-doo-doo dance around our bathroom in Cincinnati.

Weeping softly, I waited for Mom to call Jude a monster, for her to say a million times over how sorry she was for everything I endured. I needed a million apologies. I needed my mommy. The silence grew long. My eyes burned as my mother failed me yet again.

When I said I needed to go, Mom added that she also spoke with her mother, Mimi. "I told her what Jude did to you. She said that kind of thing happens in every family."

Nauseated, I sat on a step and pressed my flushed cheek to the cool wall. Mimi wasn't disturbed on my behalf? If she said it happens in every family, it probably happened to her too.

For years, I resented Mom and Dad for their continued communication with Jude. How could a parent maintain a relationship with someone who did despicable things to one of their children? Who cared if that someone was one of their other offspring?

One night after supper, when the kids went upstairs to watch a movie, I asked Chad, "What would you do if one of our kids did something terrible to one of the others?"

His brow rumpled. "I'm not sure."

"I'd grab the kid, shake him or her, and say, 'How could you?'"

"No, you wouldn't. You'd say, 'Where did we go wrong?' We both would."

I nodded. "You're probably right. I'd blame myself, or us. I'd wonder what we did or didn't do that caused it."

"And, 'How can we fix it?'" Chad added. "We'd say that too."

"I'd never stop saying to the one kid, 'I'm sorry I failed you. How can I make it up to you?'"

"But would you hate the bad kid?" Chad asked.

"I used to think I would, but honestly? I don't think I could hate my own child, no matter what."

Maybe Mom wasn't so bad after all, but those things I said I'd say? They're what I wanted for me. For Little Dina. I wanted Mom to cover me with a blanket of apologies. As for Jude, I wanted him to suffer consequences.

Years before I ordered Jude to stay away from me and my family, he visited us—Chad, Sophia, and me. At the time, we lived in Cincinnati. Sophia was two months old, and I'd recently decided to stay home with her. Originally I'd planned to go back to work, but once she arrived, I couldn't do it. I couldn't bear the thought of someone else experiencing her developmental milestones instead of me.

In the days leading up to Jude's arrival, I almost asked Chad to take vacation time so Sophia and I wouldn't have to be alone with Jude during the day. In the end I didn't say anything. It was before

Chad knew what Jude had done to me. Not knowing the details, Chad wouldn't understand how uncomfortable I felt with my own brother. Family means everything to Chad.

The first night of Jude's visit, Chad volunteered to ready Sophia for bed while I did the supper dishes. I whispered could he please buckle Sophia into her infant carrier and set her on the floor by my side of the bed? He hesitated, then agreed.

Jude showed us more than two hours of slides—images of him gallivanting around the world. Close to eleven that night, Jude drilled a throw pillow at my face. "Wake up, stupid, I'm not done!"

That did it. The latent fear I'd felt leading up to his visit became fury. I flung the pillow back. "I'm tired, jerk. Do you have any idea what it's like to wake up three to four times a night with a baby?" I stood and headed toward the stairs. On the bottom step I faced him. "Of course you don't. All you care about is you. Do you even remember the names of the Swedish girl in the hot tub or those women at the Philippine swim-up bar? My guess is no. All you give a rat's ass about is Jude, the world-traveling dude. Grow up already."

I started up the stairs, but when Jude spoke, I paused.

"You're right," he said. "You and Chad have everything—each other, a child, a home. I have nothing, not even a set of keys. Who needs keys with no car or house?"

I sneered. "Are you bragging or complaining?"

"What I mean is, it's all about family. You guys have it. I don't. You're the lucky ones."

"What, am I supposed to feel sorry for you?"

Instead of answering, Jude began to disassemble the slide projector. At the front door, Chad flipped the dead bolt and slid the chain. He told Jude to turn off the lights when he was done, then he climbed the steps behind me, his hand in the small of my back.

Late that night, I crouched beside Sophia sleeping in her carrier and vowed to protect her forever. Slipping under the covers beside Chad, I sighed as our waterbed's warmth surrounded me, but for once its gentle wave action failed to lull me to sleep. For the next hour I pondered my conversation with Jude. If the only thing he wanted was a family, why did he do the very things that prohibited it? If he got a real job, instead of working seasonal gigs like fishing in Alaska or waiting tables at ski resorts, maybe he'd attract a wife. No doubt a car would help too. What kind of thirty-something guy doesn't own a vehicle?

Snuggling against Chad, I wondered why my anger had ambushed me tonight. Where had it come from? For ten years Jude had lived far away—in states out west, if not on the opposite side of the world. The distance made me feel safe, but now he was here, invading my home as if nothing ever happened, like he was the world's best big brother and uncle. Plus, now we had Sophia. Being the mother of an infant stirred feelings in me I had never experienced before. Any threat to her, imagined or real, quickened my pulse.

Why didn't I tell him not to visit? It would've raised questions, but wasn't it time questions were raised? When he visited again—no, he would not be visiting again. After what he said about family being so important to him, I knew how to get him back for what he did. I'd cut him off from me and my family. Next time he wanted to visit, I'd say, "Nope, never again." Let him make his own family and when and if he did, God help the woman crazy enough to be his wife.

As soon as I made the decision, I felt almost boneless. Liquid. It was a relief to know I'd never have to deal with him again. Abuse issues aside, I did not enjoy his company. His tendency to dominate discussions and push his opinions on others exasperated me. I despised the way he demeaned your stance if you didn't agree with him. And his anger was fierce. An ex-girlfriend of his had confided in me, "Jude doesn't have anger issues. He has rage issues."

Also obnoxious was the way he tried to take over in the kitchen. Every evening he hovered behind me and suggested modifications to the dish I prepared—make more of it, spice it up, add tomatoes. Plus, he was a pig. For breakfast he often ate close to an entire box of cereal drenched in milk. At lunch and supper, he helped himself to seconds and thirds. It didn't seem an issue of Jude being full or not. It was more that he wanted to eat as much as possible to keep others from having any. Prior to his arrival, I relocated a significant amount of our nonperishable food items to the basement. Maybe if he didn't get enough to eat, he'd shorten his stay.

What was at the root of it all? His excessive anger, the way he took advantage of people's hospitality, and his gluttony with food and alcohol, sex and drugs? My brother Tom said it was because our parents rarely disciplined Jude. Tom believed they were soft on Jude because he was their favorite child. I thought they didn't punish Jude enough because they were afraid of him.

Jude always tried to be the proverbial alpha dog. In every setting, he attempted to gain status through charisma. If that failed, he resorted to intimidation, verbal or physical. Many times I watched his face go from handsome and confident to ugly and oppositional. Since he seemed to have an unusual respect for Chad —perhaps he sensed my husband's unwavering loyalty to me—I didn't anticipate trouble while he visited us.

The next morning after breakfast, I informed Jude that Sophia and I were going for a walk. He slipped into a windbreaker and followed us outside.

On our way to the park, I chattered to Sophia, teaching her the names of flowers along the way: tulips, daffodils, forsythia. I sang her favorite songs: "The Wheels on the Bus" and "How Much Is

That Doggie in the Window?" To force Jude to walk behind us, I rolled the stroller in the center of the sidewalk.

After lunch, as I moved to take Sophia upstairs for her nap, Jude held out his arms. Avoiding his eyes, I bounced Sophia on my shoulder and patted her back, encouraging her to burp.

"Can I hold her?"

My grip on Sophia tightened as I tried to think of a reason to refuse. The word *no* wouldn't come out so I asked if he knew how. He said of course he knew how; he'd held Mark's kids plenty of times. Yeah, and Mark was a fool to let you, I thought.

Jude came over and pried Sophia out of my arms. Focusing on her slate-colored eyes, I willed her to cry or fuss, but she did neither. When she cooed at him, my stomach rolled.

A minute later, Jude handed her back, his face contorted. "I think she pooped."

I lifted her bottom to my nose. "That's gas, silly." Nearing the top of the steps, I called down to say I needed a nap too. We'd be down later.

That night a friend from Columbus dropped by. At the end of the evening, he asked if he could crash on our sofa since he was tired and feeling the effects of a few beers. No problem, we told him.

Early the next morning on our way to the kitchen, Chad and I tiptoed past our sleeping friend on the sofa. He joined us minutes later, wearing his coat, car keys in hand.

"No need to rush off," I said. "Don't you want coffee and pancakes?"

"No, thanks. I'm going to hit the road before your brother wakes up. Last night he came downstairs and put the moves on me. Why didn't you tell me he was gay?" When our mouths fell open, he turned to go. "I know. It freaked me out too, which is why I'll be leaving now."

"Maybe he was drunk and didn't know what he was doing," I said.

Beside the front door our friend faced us. "Trust me. He knew exactly what he was doing."

CHAPTER SIX
Fear

On December 31, 1999, the world waited anxiously for the arrival of the new millennium.

Thinking there would be chaos, people stockpiled bottled water, toilet paper, canned food, and generators. Some folks, certain all the money in financial institutions everywhere would go poof the minute the clock struck midnight, emptied their bank accounts. Obscure religious cults proclaimed: "The world is going to end, for real this time!"

Chad and I weren't worried. We planned to spend the weekend with the kids in a cabin at a nearby state park.

After supper on New Year's Eve, Chad built a fire in the stone hearth, and soon the dry heat flushed our cheeks. For entertainment, the girls staged a pretend ice skating show. In matching footie pajamas, they swooped and spun around on the hardwood floor of the main room. Propped in a corner of the couch, four-month-old Wyatt chortled in amusement.

Around ten o'clock, unsure of whether we'd be awake at midnight, Chad popped open a bottle of champagne. Clinking his jelly jar against mine, he said, "*Salute,* Sunshine. It's not every day you get to experience the change of a year, a century, and a millennium."

While Chad put Wyatt to bed, the girls played with their Beanie Baby stuffed animals, and I arranged an assortment of small canvases, paints, and brushes on the dining table. Since it was such a special night, I wanted each of us to create something to commemorate the date. Sophia painted a pink and blue sunset. Chad's painting resembled a striped Venus de Milo. In neon-bright colors, Lark's proclaimed the year 2000.

I coated my canvas with black paint and in the middle, I added a child's hand with a heart in the center. On the left I painted a flame and on the right, a star. All over the canvas I dabbed yellow and orange squiggly lines to simulate radiating light. I was sure that where there was light, there was hope. But if the cabin went dark, something awful would happen. As I painted, every muscle in my body was tense and my heart raced.

As Chad helped the girls brush their teeth, I stared out into the night that straddled 1999 and 2000. Tonight would be the perfect night for a murder, I thought. The ideal occasion to kill a person. Or a family. What a way to ring in the new millennium. Maybe it would be random. The murderer might not know me, or us. Perhaps he would simply stab a spot on a map and say, "I will go there and kill." But what if it wasn't a stranger? Maybe it was someone who knew me, knew us.

Deep down, I felt certain Jude would come to kill me. What if he traveled here on this unique date to make a statement? "Because you tried to leave me out of your family, this is what happened."

I wondered if my anxiety was connected to my counseling. For months, I'd spoken with Jamie about my childhood abuse. Perhaps Jude was angry at me for telling Mom and Dad what he did, and he chose this time and place to get revenge.

I kept thinking about *Helter Skelter*, the book and movie about

Charles Manson. In high school, I'd refused to see the movie, but my best friend Katie Lynn had pestered me into peeking at the photographs in the book. I'd glanced down, gasped, and begged her to take the book away.

That night when I closed my eyes, the walls of our tiny cabin resembled those in *Helter Skelter*, except the blood spraying the walls was ours. I didn't dare confide in Chad. He might think me crazy. Or he might venture outside to inspect the surrounding area and whoever was out there would slit his throat or shoot him with a silenced gun.

Chad joined me by the picture window. Speaking into my hair, he said he was going to hit the hay, did I care to join him? I promised to be in after I washed the paintbrushes. He offered to get more firewood and moments later, he stood on the back deck. Beside the door, I waited, ready to drag him inside, if necessary. While he arranged new logs on the fire, I bolted the door. Trying to sound casual, I asked if there seemed to be people in the other cabins. He said it was too dark to tell.

Once I heard the bed creak with his weight, I flipped on the lights in the main room and kitchen. To rid the space of darkness and shadows. Working quickly, I rearranged the furniture—dragging the wood-framed sofa to the center of the living room and shoving the coffee table against the back door. Satisfied with the room's logistics, I tucked myself into a corner of the small couch, the fireplace poker in one hand and the hearth shovel in the other.

Afraid to look anywhere else, I focused on the flames. Which door would the killer use? The front door or the one in the kitchen? Or maybe he'd enter through a window. Would he kill us quickly or torture us first?

Flashing back to high school biology class, I wondered if an eviscerated human body resembled a pale, dissected frog. Picturing a sheep eye, big as a ping pong ball, I remembered how in eighth grade science class, the liquid inside had spurted a foot high when the orb was pierced. Right before my lab partner had poked it, the eyeball looked so uncaring, all skim-milk blue. Our teacher had instructed us to move quickly and with strength to puncture it on the first try.

"Stop it!" I hissed. I waited for someone to stir—Chad, the kids, him. Footsteps rustled outside, someone stomping through frost-stiff leaves. The noise sounded close to the picture window. I forced myself to turn toward it. A circle of breath clouded the glass. I sat up, arms raised, weapons ready. A black spot pierced the center of the cloud like a bull's-eye. I gripped my weapons more tightly. Two eyes peered in at me—large and brown, then eerie green, glowing.

A deer. It was only a deer.

All night I kept watch, fear thrumming in my veins like too much caffeine. I dozed off once then jerked awake, frantic that I'd slept. At last I allowed myself a glance outside. Dawn was approaching. Its torn pink edges creeping up through the evergreens. Jude didn't show. We didn't die.

I stood and stretched, then returned my weapons to their stand on the hearth and the furniture to its previous location. Slipping into the kids' room, I straightened Wyatt's blanket and smiled at the girls sprawled across the bed, their limbs flopped over one another. Sophia stirred, but Lark lay so still that I stepped closer and hovered my hand an inch above her mouth to make sure she was breathing.

In our bedroom across the hall, I collapsed next to Chad. As I spooned against him, my hot tears wet his back.

The next week in therapy, I recounted my weekend to Jamie. "What do you think it means?" I asked.

Jamie tapped a front tooth with her pen. "I think it's a combination of things. All the hype leading up to the new millennium, much of it fearful. And the work you and I are doing, that probably had something to do with it as well. Plus, your abuse always happened at night, in the dark, right?" Jamie's eyes widened. "Question. I can't believe I didn't think of this before. Are you still scared of him?"

In my chair, I winced. She was right.

In 1993, when Chad, Sophia, and I moved back to West Virginia, my paranoia significantly increased. I knew sooner or later Jude would visit Mom and Dad. For decades they had lived in my childhood home, three and a half hours away from where we now lived, but recently they'd relocated to be closer to me and my family. We could drive to their new house, or vice versa, in under an hour. If Jude visited them, he'd be quite close to me and my family. Too close.

Sometimes I imagined Jude outside our house, peeking in windows like he used to. There were days when I thought twice about letting the girls play outside. What if he snatched one or both of them? Or maybe he'd expose himself, another trick of his.

While Jude and I still lived at home, some mornings I would need to go into the attic. To access the storage area, I needed to go through Jude's room. When I did, he was always asleep—or pretending to be. More often than not, he was naked, with the covers tumbled down near the footboard. As I stepped into his room, there it would be, his erection. I hurried through the attic door, casting my eyes down and to the right so I didn't have to see it, the way it bounced in an almost jaunty way. When I left the attic, I'd hold my summer or winter clothing box beside my head to block the view.

Other times he barged into the second-floor bathroom as I showered. He'd half-heartedly apologize as he peered through the glass door, claiming he thought I was Tom. I'd turn my back and scream for Mom.

Always, always, Jude was in search of sexual stimulation. For this reason, I frequently scoured internet lists of sex offenders for his name. When I couldn't find it, I figured it was simply a matter of time. Because Jude couldn't not do what he did. Knowing that, there was no way I'd allow him near my kids.

I returned to my session with Jamie. "You're right. I am still afraid of him. But more for my kids' sake than mine. Honestly, I don't ever want to see him again. But someday it's bound to happen, right? Someone in our family will die, Mimi or Aunt Peg, and I'll run into him at their funeral. I hope it doesn't happen anytime soon, because the thought of seeing him scares the pee out of me."

CHAPTER SEVEN
Art Therapy

JAMIE AND I SPENT THE NEXT TWO SESSIONS DISCUSSING CHAD'S habit of not talking to me for two or three days at a time whenever I said or did something that pissed him off. Jamie called this caveman behavior. I told her it wasn't that big of a deal. All I had to do to restore peace was apologize.

She snorted. "Why would you apologize if you're not wrong?"

"Because it's easy."

"Easy isn't always better. Negative behavior without negative consequences will never change. That's Psychology 101."

This had become my habit of late, bringing Jamie issues from the present to distract her from picking apart my past. I was afraid to go deeper, scared of what I might find. Sometimes when we talked about Jude, Jamie videotaped my descriptions, complete with my flushed face and runny nose. At the end of those appointments, she'd hand me the tape and tell me to watch it at home. She said my brain needed to process the abuse so it could heal.

I never watched the tapes. They were hidden in a box in the basement.

That day, toward the end of my appointment, Jamie announced

our work together was winding down. For her sake, I pushed out my lower lip and whimpered.

She moved toward the door and waited for me to follow. We walked down the beige hallway to enter a room with a sign that read "Art Therapy." Brightly lit by a wall of windows, it was a conference room. In the center, chairs surrounded a long table covered with a canvas drop cloth. At one end of the room stood shelves filled with jars of paint, bottles of glue, colored pencils, and crayon boxes. Big rolls of blank paper leaned against the walls.

Jamie recommended that I spend a few days in art therapy. I walked over to the shelf where works in progress were displayed: paintings, collages, dioramas.

"Doing what?" I asked.

"Whatever you want. Draw, paint, make a poster of your life. Other clients will be in here with you, working on their projects, so it's kind of like group therapy. I think you'll know what to do."

On the floor beneath a window, I spied a white plastic tub of clay. "I know exactly what to make."

My first day in the art room, I found an empty chair and hung my jean jacket across the back. Over by the window, I got a sizable hunk of clay and returned to my seat. I didn't feel comfortable joining the conversation right off, so I stayed quiet to learn everyone else's stories.

As I shaped my clay, the people around me chatted. I learned that the older lady seated at the head of the table had witnessed a car wreck. With manicured fingers, she adjusted the collar of her blouse as she explained how watching the accident from the berm gave her post-traumatic stress disorder. I was pretty sure she just wanted attention and was able to pay $90 an hour to get it.

I estimated the gal in the chair across from me to be twenty or twenty-two. For the longest time she didn't speak. She was a big girl, and despite the width of the table between us, my sensitive nose determined she needed a shower. When her lips began moving with no sound, I held up my hand to shush the conversation in the room. "Say it again," I told her, "louder."

Her voice was still weak. "If I get huge, maybe they won't want me no more."

"Who won't?"

Her gnawed nails traced the tabletop. "The bad men. They tie me up. Cram a rag in my mouth. Drive me to the cabin way out in the woods." Her last sentence was a whisper. "Ever since I was four."

My fists flattened my sculpture. "Who are they? Where are they? I'll kill them. Cut off their—"

She cringed at my outburst and began to cry, her green eyes turning muddy. Then she bowed her head and gripped her midsection, rocking and softly humming.

The second version of my statue was smaller, because that's how my issue seemed to me after hearing hers.

"Why do I need to go with you today?" Chad asked three weeks later.

"It's kind of like I'm graduating," I said. "From art therapy." I sent him to the basement for his hammer. He hesitated, one eyebrow raised. I snapped my fingers and told him to move it or we'd be late.

At the clinic, Jamie waited for us inside the door. Chad introduced himself and thanked her for all the help she'd given me. She hugged him quickly, then the two of them followed me to the art room where I greeted my therapy buddies.

I positioned Chad at one end of the table and asked Jamie to bring me the trash can. At the works-in-progress shelf, I collected my project—an oversized penis—and toted it to the table. As I set it down between Chad and me, I watched the blood drain from his face.

"Don't worry. It's Jude's, and just for the record, this is not life-sized, but I got tired of starting over. His is way—" Chad pressed his finger to my lips.

Jamie asked if I'd prepared a speech. I reached into my pocket, drew out a small scrap of paper, and waved it high. When I elbowed Chad, he placed his hammer on the table in front of me.

I glanced around the table to make sure everyone was ready, then cleared my throat. "Jude, I hate what you did to me all those years, but you no longer have power over me. I have the power now. The power is mine." The words seemed strong in my mouth. I liked the way they jarred the stillness in the room.

With both hands I lifted the hammer and brought it down hard on the statue. Clay chunks and bits flew everywhere. I continued to smash the phallus until it was demolished. Near the edge of the table, I piled up clay parts and dust. Tipping the trash can, I swept the mess inside.

Jamie and the others began to clap and one guy whistled. The big girl dabbed at her eyes. As the applause ended, I thanked my friends and wished them all the best. I left with a larger, fuller heart.

CHAPTER EIGHT
Bodywork

AT THE END OF OUR FINAL APPOINTMENT, JAMIE HANDED ME THE business card of a therapist who specialized in bodywork.

"Bodywork," Jamie explained, "is any form of therapy in which parts of the body are manipulated. Many patients who've experienced trauma benefit from bodywork. I hope you do too."

During my first day with Ruth, she instructed me to stand in the middle of the room and sink roots deep into the soil of the earth, like a tree. She reminded me of a garden gnome without the pointy hat, so her request did not surprise me. My toes felt as if they were kneading bread as I pretended to be one of the fifty-foot evergreen trees that flanked the front of my house. Ruth then told me to send my roots deeper. She claimed the exercise would make me feel grounded, but at the end of the session, I felt no different.

The second time we met, Ruth and I faced each other in matching leather chairs. She explained that the day's goal was to locate my third eye. I waited for her to grin and say she was kidding, but she didn't. Several times I reached up to tap the spot between my eyebrows.

"It's not actually there, Dina. It's in your mind."

After that appointment, on the way to my car, I plucked petals off an imaginary daisy. "Go back next week. Don't go. Go back next week. Don't."

The next time we met, Ruth led me into the spacious room beside her office. A variety of pillows were scattered on the floor. Ruth closed the door and handed me a tennis racket. "Pretend like the pillows are Jude," she said. "Take out your anger on them. Don't hold back."

Tightly gripping the handle of the racket, I pictured myself on the high school tennis team. I battered the cushions with forehands, backhands, and overhead kill shots. This activity was almost as satisfying as bludgeoning my sculpture in art therapy. I continued to whack at the pillow pile until Ruth declared time's up.

The following week, she led me back to the same room, dimmed the lights, and instructed me to lie on the carpeted floor. "Imagine you're in your childhood bedroom. It's the middle of the night. Jude just entered your room. This time, don't act like you're asleep."

Suddenly my bladder felt uncomfortably full—a water balloon beneath my belly button. A wad of soggy tissues lodged in my throat made it difficult to swallow.

This time was different, Ruth assured me. Her voice was almost a shout. "For once you're not frozen with fear. You're strong, Dina. And you have a voice. Now use it!"

When she said that, I felt larger than the room. I swung my fists at the air and shouted until my throat burned. I paused for a moment. Could people hear me? The customers in the bookstore downstairs, the students in the beauty school next door? I decided I didn't care. I screamed for, then at my parents, my whole family. "I. Hate. You. All!" I slammed both hands over my mouth. You shouldn't say those kinds of things to your parents, I thought. And you shouldn't hate your family.

For several minutes I lay still. As the air conditioning evaporated my sweat, my heartbeat slowed. Cussing my family might be bad, but it sure felt good.

When I stood, Ruth nodded approval and handed me a towel. Without a word, I wiped my face and arms, gave her my check, and left. Behind me, I heard the patter of her slippers on hardwood, and her thin voice asking about our next appointment. Same time, week after next, I spoke over my shoulder.

All the way home, a Mona Lisa smile stayed on my lips.

A month later as I settled into the chair across from Ruth, she chirped, "What's new?"

I shrugged as I nudged my cuticles back with a car key. I told her my thoughts had changed recently.

She leaned forward and asked exactly how had they changed.

"I don't know why, but for the past few days, I've been thinking I don't want to talk about the past anymore. I'm ready for something different, something new."

She made a little humming noise and suggested we explore my thoughts. While we explored, I wondered if she could tell I was bored with bodywork, sick of sitting in her office, tired of handing her checks. I longed to start my life over—better, brand new—without her or anyone else's help.

Behind her desk, Ruth stirred the various paper piles, occasionally lifting an item to peer underneath. "Surely this whole difficulty has strained your marriage. I think you and Chad would benefit from some sessions together." She held out a business card. "Nick's great. He counsels couples. Tell him I sent you."

Within five minutes of meeting Nick, I did not like him. When we joined him on his front porch, why did he shake hands with Chad and not me? All he gave me was a curt nod. His habit of blinking too often, as if he couldn't handle sustained eye contact, made me distrust him. Did he have a terrible secret? Then there was the petroleum odor of his gleaming black hair. And a voice that sounded as if it came from a small closet behind his nostrils.

Right then I should have grabbed Chad's hand and said, "I've changed my mind. Let's go." But the truth was, I still hoped someone could make my life better, fuller and happier, the way it was before all the remembering began.

As we walked through the dining room, Nick gestured to a teenaged boy seated at the table with textbooks spread all around. "Troy, tell the nice people hello." Troy sneered.

Nick led us downstairs, through the laundry room, and into his office. The tricolor carpet reeked as if a dog, or Troy, had peed on it. I took in the dated paneling and the triangle of brown metal folding chairs. If Nick was such a good therapist, why couldn't he afford a real office with decent furniture?

I don't remember what we talked about during the first session. Maybe Nick said we were getting to know each other. Whatever. The second appointment was also unremarkable until, lifting cupped hands, Nick asked Chad and me to stand. Once we were up, he held his hands parallel, as if he were about to clap.

"Move closer," he murmured. "Facing one another."

We shuffled closer—Chad grinning, me giggling.

"Now, Chad, kiss Dina." My hands balled into fists and my arms stiffened. Nick crept in a circle around us. "I want to observe how the two of you interact."

As soon as Chad stepped toward me, his hands out as if he might rest them on my waist, I scrambled backward, windmilling my arms to keep from falling. "Stop it! I don't want to." I whipped around to face Nick, my eyes wild. I jabbed the air near his face with my pointer finger. "Ever since this whole thing started—all this crap, all these Jude memories—I haven't been able to kiss Chad on the mouth. Not once. Not ever. And now you want me to do it in front of you? I don't think so." I seized Chad's wrist and tugged him toward the laundry room.

Nick darted in front of us, his hands up. "Okay, okay. I have another idea. Come back next week."

I pressed him for details. It would have to be a great idea for me to give him another chance.

"EFT," he said. "Emotional Freedom Technique. I've had considerable success with it."

I asked how it worked.

"It involves tapping various parts of the body while thinking about the issues that concern you."

I snickered. "Tapping? Really?"

"As I said, I've experienced considerable success with this technique."

"How much is it?"

His fingers twitched, as if he was counting. "Five thousand dollars should cover the cost."

I gawked but Chad did not. "Whatever it takes," he said under his breath. "I just want you to get better."

I recalled that while working with Jamie, she used a technique called EMDR—eye movement desensitization and reprocessing. She wiggled her finger, and I focused on it while retrieving memories. Sometimes it worked, sometimes it didn't. Either way, she never charged me extra for it.

I faced Nick. "Give me the names of the people you've had 'considerable success' with." I scratched quotation marks in the air.

Nick shook his head fervently. "I can't do that. It would be an invasion of their privacy." He moved toward the door. "Think about it and give me a call if you wish to proceed."

Two weeks later, I pounded on Ruth's door.

She opened it a crack and squinted up at me. "You're angry."

I brushed past her to my chair. "Darn right, I'm angry. That creepy lizard friend of yours wanted to do some bizarre procedure —tapping and snapping—to the tune of $5,000. He assured us it would make all my memories 'tabula rasa,' clean slate. He thinks he can make all the bad stuff in my brain disappear just like that. And yet, he won't extend a money-back guarantee or provide us the names and numbers of people who have experienced his great miracle. Oh please! If he was that good, he would've been on Oprah by now." I scowled at Ruth. "Did you know he'd do that when you sent us there? Are you getting a kickback?"

Ruth gaped at me, her tiny gnome eyes bulging. As she shook her head vehemently, her steely bobbed hair swung back and forth. "I'm sorry. I had no ..." Her powdery voice trailed off but her lips kept moving. She was a small pitiful fish.

I dried my palms on my jeans. "You know what? I'm done. Done with counseling. Have a nice life."

CHAPTER NINE
Church

At supper one evening, Chad asked if I ever noticed the little church at the four-way stop by the girls' grade school.

"The white one with the red doors?" I said.

He nodded. "We should try it someday. Going to church."

I wrinkled my nose. "Why?"

"You went when you were little. I did too. It'd be good for the kids, don't you think?"

I didn't tell Chad that when I was in junior high, after a lifetime of attending church, I decided I didn't want anything more to do with religion. In fact, one night after youth group I actually told God, "I believe in you and most of the stuff in the Bible, but I can't have fun with all those rules. I want to live my way. I'll get back to you, though, I promise. Right before I die, okay?"

God didn't answer.

"It's a Methodist church," Chad said. "Not Catholic like I was raised, or Presbyterian like you were."

I shrugged. "Fine. We can try it."

The next Sunday as we drove home from church, Sophia informed us she loved how the pastor resembled Santa Claus and that animal crackers had been the Sunday school snack. "Animals were on the ark, you know."

The service had reminded me of my childhood church: Stand and sing. Sit down for the sermon. Pray. Sing again. Pass the offering plate. Sing the benediction: "Praise God from whom all blessings flow ..." Nothing had changed except now I was too old to sketch horses when I was bored. But that morning when we sang hymns, I hardly had to look at the hymnal. I still remembered the songs.

From that day forward, we attended church most Sundays. Because I enjoyed the singing, the new friends we made, and the weekly ritual of worship. Chad did too. Within a few months, the woman who coordinated the Sunday school program asked me to teach Vacation Bible School. Not long after, the pastor invited Chad to serve on a couple of committees.

One Sunday, Mrs. Wise, the leader of the silver-haired ladies, suggested I bring some social event ideas to the next outreach meeting. At the meeting, the ladies approved all my plans—Valentine's party, field trip to a local passion play, and an ice cream social.

The Valentine's party was well attended. Afterward, Mrs. Wise asked how the sign-up was going for the passion play outing. When I told her fifty people were signed up, her face brightened. "That's more than half the congregation," she said. As we walked to our cars, she patted my shoulder. "How nice it is to have fresh ideas in the church."

The night of the passion play, I settled the members of our congregation in their seats in the high school auditorium, then sat down next to Chad.

For the next two hours, I watched the Bible—specifically, the Easter story—come to life. I knew the story well. More than once, I'd read the words on the page. On at least a dozen Easter mornings, I heard the story told. But that night, it was as if I witnessed Jesus himself teaching, performing miracles, and dying on a cross. And now on the stage in front of me, I watched his return, resplendent and glorious.

Soon after, the crowd stood to leave but then sat back down when a young man appeared onstage with a microphone. "Good evening, everyone. On behalf of Grace Community Church, I want to thank you for attending tonight's production. We hope you saw something you can believe in."

As the seats around me emptied, and even Chad started up the aisle, I continued to stare at the last place I'd seen Jesus. Perched on the edge of my seat with my hands pressed together, I felt split open like a seed when it sprouts a root.

Before I stood to go, I whispered into the space between my palms: "I believe."

CHAPTER TEN
Change

That fall, I woke early one Saturday. Chad's back was to me, covered by the sheet. He didn't respond when I tapped his shoulder. I wanted to tell him the dark was gone, my dark. I hadn't mentioned to him that for the last year, maybe two, I'd felt wrapped in cotton. Thick and indigo, the fabric held me fast and made it difficult to take a satisfactory breath.

An image of Snow White lying in a see-through coffin entered my mind. She appeared to be dead, but I knew she was sleeping. It was like I'd been asleep too, for the longest time. Now that the grogginess was gone, I was ready to escape confinement and run free.

I flipped the sheet's hem, and cool air wafted over us. Chad stirred.

"Are you awake?" I whispered.

"I am now."

When I described how I felt like Snow White, he rolled to face me.

"Does that mean I'm Prince Charming?" His grin was silly and hopeful.

I rubbed at the sleep crease below his eye. "I'm not sure. I haven't figured that part out yet."

One evening as I passed through our family room, Chad caught me by the wrist and pulled me onto the love seat. He pointed to the television and suggested I watch. Arranging the faux fur blanket over our laps, he explained it was a documentary on religious zealots. People like me.

I twisted away. "I am not a zealot. Those people are nuts!"

He held me tight when I tried to stand. "Okay, so zealot's not the right word. What I'm trying to say is you've changed. You don't cuss anymore. You've stopped telling dirty jokes." I told him I had to, because of the kids.

"I know, but remember the time in Cincinnati when you won that citywide dirty joke-telling contest?" I covered my face and groaned. "Plus you're nicer to your mom now. Well, sometimes. And you started a youth group at church. Like I said, it's not a bad thing."

I shoved the blanket to the floor and stood. "Whatever. Oh, and you forgot one. I also organized a Bible study."

For months I couldn't go anywhere without seeing the name of the church that performed the passion play—Grace Community Church. One of their banners near the college campus read: "Experience God, not religion." I stared at the sentence as I waited for the traffic light to change. Experience God. What would that be like? Would I be able to hear his voice? Or maybe see his face without going blind?

At supper that night I told Chad my Bible study gal pals raved about the music and sermons at Grace Community Church.

"Let's try it then."

"But ... we can't just leave our church," I said. "We're members now. We should be loyal, shouldn't we? To the church and to Pastor Dan?"

Chad arched an eyebrow. "What about to God?"

Later that night I thought about Chad's question and wished I'd thought of it. Each time I spotted another sign for Grace Community Church, I remembered Chad's words. Perhaps wanting more of God was a good enough reason to try another church.

The Sunday after September 11, 2001, our little church was standing room only. After the initial hymn, Pastor Dan assumed his place behind the pulpit. From our seats two rows back, his knuckles resembled white marbles. It was odd to see him without a smile, with no twinkle in his eye. When at last he spoke, he confessed he didn't know what to say.

I inched closer to Chad and reached for his hand. We waited for Pastor Dan to say something else, but he didn't. Wasn't there a verse he could read? I wondered. Surely the Bible spoke about what to do in difficult times. Eventually our pastor stepped away from the podium and sank onto the bench in front of the choir loft. After a few minutes, the music director played a solemn song and folks began to leave.

That night at supper Chad asked if the passion play church offered a Sunday night service. An hour later, we sat inside Grace Community Church beside Bobbi, a friend of mine from Bible study. Chad glanced around the large windowless room. Where's the altar, he wanted to know. I was curious why there were padded chairs instead of pews. Bobbi smiled as she explained that Grace Community was a contemporary church, not a traditional one.

The songs we sang were not traditional either, but I loved them. Chad whispered he could get used to this kind of church. After the music ended, a trim man wearing jeans and a dress shirt climbed onto the stage and arranged his Bible and notes on the lectern.

"Tonight we have reason to be hopeful," he said. Reciting a number of scriptures, the pastor encouraged us to not be afraid.

Chad and I held hands and every time the preacher said something we liked, one or both of us squeezed hard.

More than once during the following week, Chad mentioned how much he liked the service at Grace Community Church. Each time, I said, "Me too." Soon after, we began attending Grace Community on Sunday evenings after supper, in addition to going to our little white church on Sunday mornings.

One night as we drove down Grace Community's long driveway, I said, "It might sound mean, but when we go to church on Sunday mornings, it feels like dry toast, but when we come here—"

Chad nodded. "I know. I feel the same. Should we switch?"

"I think so, but not yet."

CHAPTER ELEVEN
The F-Word

During counseling, I had asked Jamie and Ruth the same question: "Do I have to forgive Jude?" No, they both said. This was about me, not him. Part of me wanted to believe them, but another part thought they might be wrong.

One afternoon I stepped onto the front porch for the mail and tripped over a thick paperback Bible. A Post-it note stuck to the front cover read: *"Remember how you said you wanted to read through the Bible? Try this one. It's chronological, with all the events in the order they happened. Love, Bobbi."*

As I took the book inside, a thought occurred to me. Maybe reading through the Bible would show me whether or not I should forgive Jude.

By the time I read through the entire Bible, over a year had passed, and dozens of paper slivers marked passages—Old Testament and New—regarding forgiveness. Still not convinced, I silently suggested to God that he show me about the topic. In real life.

The following Sunday morning, Pastor Dan posed a question from the pulpit. "How many times must we forgive a brother who offends us?"

I glanced around to see if anyone else was fidgeting. Had he actually said, "brother?" Pastor Dan then answered his own question. "The answer is seven times seventy." In my seat, I sagged.

Two days later I drove to Bobbi's house for Bible study. As she loaded the videotaped lesson into the player, the other ladies and I helped ourselves to coffee. As I cradled my pottery mug, Bobbi's best friend, Deborah, leaned across the table. "Dina, I have a word for you."

I smiled. "What word is that?"

The ladies all grinned as Bobbi explained that Deborah wanted to give me a message from the Lord. I huddled against the back of the chair, shielding my heart with my coffee cup. "She can do that?"

Deborah's eyes were blue stained glass, and I was certain they could see inside of me. "As soon as you walked into the room, I had a vision." With her eyes closed, she continued. "I see you with your brother, the one you haven't talked to in years, and you two are hugging." I set my mug on the table with a thud, and Deborah opened her eyes. "Does that mean something to you?"

Figuring God would tell her if I lied, I nodded. In a hoarse voice I asked if she could see the future. "It's not like that," she said. "I only see what God shows me. Do you want to talk about it?" I shook my head and told her no, thanks.

After Bible study, I drove up the hill and parked in front of our house. Deborah saw me hugging Jude? That was impossible. Hugging him would require forgiving him, and I didn't plan on doing that anytime soon. Maybe I would when Mom and Dad were dead. Maybe.

I spoke to God as if he sat in the passenger seat. "I know what you want me to do, but let me tell you why I won't. Because I hate him. If I heard he was dead, I'd be relieved. The world would be safer if he wasn't in it."

I peeked out the window to see if anybody was around. Nobody.

I then confessed to God that I felt like the memory of what Jude did to me was keeping me alive. If I let it go—I pictured myself releasing the string of a balloon in a wide-open field and watching the red sphere disappear in the clouds—I'd be like that balloon. Gone. With the wind.

I opened the glove box for a fast-food napkin. "If I don't remember, God, who will?" I soaked the paper with one blow of my nose. "And what if I do forgive him? Will everybody expect me to like him again? Maybe even love him? No way."

As I walked up the front steps, I told God I wanted Jude to pay for what he did. Every single day I hoped Jude felt as miserable as me.

CHAPTER TWELVE
Going, Going...

THE TREES BEGAN DROPPING THEIR LEAVES ABOUT THE TIME MY father started losing his mind. I didn't notice it at first. Mom, either. But Chad had recognized the change in Dad the last time we went out to eat with my parents. Dad was less social. He avoided answering questions. When Chad asked what Dad thought about a current event, he'd asked what Chad thought about it.

I remembered that night at the restaurant. We'd stood outside on the sidewalk waiting for the hostess to call our name. The late afternoon heat shimmered the air, and the fragrance of biscuits baking mingled with the pungent odor of hot blacktop. Dad elbowed me and asked who those kids were over there. I followed his line of sight. "Dad, they're your grandchildren." At the time it alarmed me, but then the hostess announced our table was ready, and I forgot about it.

By spring, Daddy's clever, three-college-degree mind was waning. Mom said he visited the bank and post office every day because he didn't remember that he'd gone the day before. Sometimes he drove down streets the wrong way, batting at Mom's hands when she tried to take the wheel. One day he yelled at her so loudly in the grocery store, the manager came over to check on them.

Whenever Chad and I visited with the kids, Dad asked what time it was every few minutes.

Mom called one afternoon and in a sharp voice said, "Mark thinks your father needs to see a doctor about his forgetfulness, but—"

"Mom, Mark's right. Dad absolutely should be tested. There may be a medicine that can help him."

Dad's appointment confirmed our suspicions. Dementia had begun, probably Alzheimer's, though Dad's doctor said only an autopsy could determine that for sure. He told Mom there was no telling whether Dad's decline would be fast or slow. Some patients held on to a fair amount of function for as long as seven years. Others failed sooner.

I counted on my fingers. "So if it's 2002 right now, and he has seven years, that means he maybe has until 2009. What then? Will he die, be bedridden, or what?"

Mom said she couldn't remember; she should've taken notes. "Also, the doctor asked Paul to surrender his driver's license." I gasped. "He didn't even argue. He took out his wallet and handed it over."

"If he did that, he must know something's wrong, that he's losing his memory and will probably end up like Granny."

In her final years, Dad's feisty mother no longer recognized any of us, not even her sons. Her eyes were cloudy skies, and the only vocalization she made was an eerie, high-pitched keen. Visiting her in the nursing home was like sitting with a ghost.

Mom filled Dad's prescription, but in time, it became clear the drug wasn't working. I told Chad we should visit Mom and Dad more often, every other weekend instead of once a month. Mom needed help. Dad did so much around the house—paid the bills, maintained the cars, balanced the checkbook, cut the grass. After more than forty years of Dad taking care of Mom, she'd have to take care of him now.

Thankfully, it only took Chad and me forty or so minutes to drive to their house. Mark lived two hours away and tried to come up every other month with his wife, Valerie. Unfortunately, Jude and Tom lived too far away to be of much help. When he was in the United States, Jude lived mostly in Colorado. Tom was in California and only visited every ten years, if that.

On one of our visits to my parents' house, Mom led Chad and me into the garage and asked if we wanted Dad's NordicTrack machine. She worried Dad would fall if he tried to use it again. Chad said sure, so Mom moved toward the shelves that lined one wall and began to sort through stacks of paper in search of the manual.

Back at home, Chad reassembled the NordicTrack in our basement. For nearly a month, whenever Wyatt was napping, I donned exercise clothes and hopped on the machine. One afternoon as I worked out, Jude came to mind along with the usual associated memories. As I reviewed my list of reasons to hate him, my f-word —forgiveness—dropped into my brain like bread into a toaster.

What would it feel like to forgive Jude? If forgiveness was what God wanted, maybe it was what was best for me. Perhaps life would be easier if I gave in to forgiveness. Sweat burned my eyes. I wiped my face but my vision was still blurry. Not with sweat, though. With tears.

I suddenly sensed a large stone resting on my shoulders. What was this weight? Shame? Anger? Take it away, God. I shut my eyes and pictured the little blue engine from my favorite childhood story. Perhaps if I believed I could get rid of the rock, I could.

I imagined shoving the boulder off a mountain. When Wyatt was born, I pushed so hard during delivery, the blood vessels in my eyes burst. I'd push that hard this time, maybe harder. I think I can.

I think I can. I imagined the rock leaving my shoulders and falling, falling. Shaking the ground when it landed. Rock dust and fragments flew everywhere.

I want it gone! The boulder sprang over the cliff. Though I didn't hear the wind from its fall, I knew I was free. I felt weightless, as if I'd let go of suitcases so heavy, I might float up in the air. If I spoke, would my voice be helium high?

For a few minutes I was afraid to move. If I resumed life, the boulder might return.

When I finally climbed the stairs, I marveled how simple forgiveness had been. Why hadn't I done it sooner?

PART TWO
The Hidden
1963–1985

CHAPTER THIRTEEN
Charlotte's Web

WHEN I WAS LITTLE, NO ONE EVER EXPLAINED MY MOTHER'S mental health issues to me. Over the years, though, I collected random information regarding her condition. One night in North Carolina, for instance.

After my college graduation in 1985, I relocated to Charlotte. My intention had always been to leave West Virginia and never return except maybe for an occasional holiday. Maybe. A few days before my move, Dad and Mom offered to drive down with me to help find an apartment and settle in. We packed my car and theirs with things I loved and supplies Mom insisted I needed, then headed south.

I'm guessing the thing that triggered Mom was Dad and me excluding her from our conversations. She seemed to think we had some kind of secret society. Really, that wasn't far from the truth. It wasn't that we planned it—or maybe we did, though never with words—but Dad and I enjoyed a strong connection. Possibly because I was the baby of our family. Maybe because I was the only girl. Either way, there were no such ties binding Mom and me.

So maybe that night in Charlotte when Dad and I fell into

another conversation that didn't include her, Mom decided she'd fix us. As we drove back to the motel after supper, I could tell she was peeved because she didn't speak. She just puffed on her cigarette and scowled out the window. It wasn't out of the ordinary, so I ignored it. But these were warning signs.

At the motel, Mom snatched the room key and scurried off while Dad and I retrieved our overnight bags from the trunk of my Toyota. When we reached the room, Dad turned the doorknob, but the door wouldn't open. He tried again, then tapped the door with the car key. He put his shoulder to it and shoved. "Come on, Jean, let us in." After five minutes, he said he was going to the office.

I thought he'd bring back a duplicate key. Or the manager. Instead, he simply paid for another room. It only surprised me a little. Dad had a habit of covering things up. Like when I used to clean Houdini's cage. Sometimes I got rid of all the dirty shavings, but other times I just heaped new ones on top of the old, hoping no one would see or smell the mess underneath. But Mom was no hamster.

Inside our room, Dad stretched out on the bed nearest the bathroom. He removed his black-framed glasses, laid them on the bedside table, and stared at the ceiling.

Burning up from the climb to the third floor, I cranked the air conditioner to high. I folded down the plasticky floral quilt, sprawled on the sheet's cool white surface, and wondered if Mom had always been weird. "What was Mom like when you met her?"

Dad massaged the bridge of his nose. "She was pretty, like you. Same blue eyes and curly dark hair. She was funny too, always playing practical jokes on her sisters." Dad smiled at the memory. "When I met her, she was in nursing school. I stole her away from a fellow she was going steady with."

I tried to picture Mom, looking like me in a white uniform,

wearing one of those blocky white hats nurses wore in the old days. I shut my eyes and imagined her flirting with Dad before he grew the beard that made him resemble Honest Abe. Mom had two guys vying for her affection? She was funny? My friends liked Mom. They said she was cute and nice. But I didn't bring friends home much because I never knew what I'd find.

Often when I walked in the door after school, she wouldn't be dressed yet. Draped in one of her blue flowered muumuu-like housecoats, she'd be stretched out on the scratchy olive-green sofa with her delicate ankles crossed. I will say one thing, no matter how big she got, her legs were always svelte.

Most of the time I veered right to go through the dining room and kitchen to get to my bedroom. That way, I didn't have to talk to her, or be reminded of her perpetual lethargy. Mom—I'd say to myself—why don't you get dressed and take a walk around the block? That might help with your ongoing weight-loss efforts.

I balanced on my elbow to face Dad. "You all fought so much. Why didn't you divorce her?"

Dad didn't speak, but I was pretty sure I knew his answer. He'd say something about loyalty, or the till-death-do-us-part wedding words. When he finally looked over at me, in his expression I saw, "If I wasn't around, do you really think she'd survive?"

Immediately, Mom's stash of sunset-colored pill bottles came to mind. Did Dad think maybe she'd dump out all the meds, shovel them into her mouth, wash them down with a half glass of Tab, and go to sleep forever? I doubted the possibility, but perhaps he wasn't so sure.

It seemed noble for him to stay, but part of me wished he'd escaped.

If I could choose my own mom, I'd ask for a cute, skinny mom like Carol Brady on *The Brady Bunch*. Or Katie Lynn's mother,

Gail. Gail's hair and eyes were the color of strong coffee and she was trim. Her outfits were always chic. If that wasn't enough, I adored the way her Southern accent spilled out like Hershey's chocolate syrup.

Every room in their house, every meal Gail prepared was flawless. Gail cooked everything from scratch. There were no canned biscuits and no instant mashed potatoes in Gail's kitchen. My favorite meal of hers was crab epicurean: a creamy and delicious seafood casserole topped with buttery toasted breadcrumbs. My mom would've served the entrée in her ancient stained Pyrex casserole dish. Gail presented it in pink clamshells the size of your hand.

In their beautiful dining room with a hand-painted mural on one wall, Katie Lynn's stepdad frequently told terrible jokes that were mean to women or Black people, and while I hated that, I never turned down Gail's invitations to supper.

Mom and Gail both worked as registered nurses. For a while they worked together at the nearby state mental hospital. When Gail assured me Mom was an excellent nurse, I assumed she was being kind. I couldn't imagine Mom being competent at anything.

I turned to see if Dad was still awake, then said something to wake him if he wasn't. "I always hated to call you at work, but she made me. She couldn't handle it when the boys fought, especially when they threw furniture." Dad let out a raggedy sigh. "She's manic-depressive, right?"

Dad sat up then, his eyes squinty. "How'd you know that?"

"Tom told me. He figured it out in in his Psychology 101 class at college."

On his bed, Dad burped softly. "Psychology class, eh?" Dad taught psychology at the local university. It perplexed me how out in the world, my father was considered a psychology expert, but at home he seemed anything but.

Dad rolled off the bed and went to brush his teeth. In front of the dresser in his undershirt and khakis, he smoothed his hair and beard. His hair was black, but his beard was beginning to silver.

Before he shut off the bedside lamp, he patted my shoulder. "Night, night. Don't let the bedbugs bite."

In the dark, I tried to keep Dad awake so we could talk more. "Remember the time the police arrested Jude for shoplifting and they shaved his head to shame him? Or did you take him to the barbershop to have his head buzzed?"

"Did I ever tell you about the high-speed chase he had with the police at Myrtle Beach?" Dad's voice was soft with sleep. "On his motorcycle? I had to drive down and bail him out. That boy's a pain in my ass."

He's a pain in everyone's ass, Dad.

When I woke the next morning, Dad was dressed. "Remember the times I took your mother to the hospital and she stayed for a week or ten days? We always called those episodes 'medication reevaluations,' but really they were nervous breakdowns."

I nodded. As far back as I could remember, I knew something was wrong with Mom. No one else's mother went into the hospital for a week at a time unless they had a baby or an operation.

Mom always seemed fine when we were out in public, like during our weekly trips to the grocery store where she and I had a ritual. Every week in the bakery section, she invited me to choose something from the glass case. Usually I requested a cream horn. The ones at the Big Bear were as big as toilet paper tubes. If I got filling on my face, she'd spit on a tissue and dab it off. That's one of my favorite memories of her—the cream horn part, not the spitty Kleenexes.

Maybe it was more that Mom acted fine when she was around people that weren't family. Sometimes she invited ladies over to play bridge. Before they arrived, we'd straighten the house, then she'd ask me to fetch her cut crystal bowls from the china closet.

She poured Chex party mix in one and chocolate bridge mix in the other. Whenever I tried to sneak some of the bridge mix, she slapped at my hand. "You're eating all the ones with the nuts," she said. So what if I did? With Mom around, there would always be enough nuts.

CHAPTER FOURTEEN
Father Knows Best... Or Not

My earliest memory is of my father, and the way he used to toss me in the air every evening when he arrived home from work. To keep from going too high, I always clutched at the collar of his white dress shirt. When I felt my hair brush the ceiling, my lower lip trembled, and I began to cry. Gently, Dad gathered me close until my chest was flush with his. His wiry beard tickled my neck as my fingers found his collarbone.

"There, there, Honey Pot," Dad said as he stroked my back. "Everything'll be all right."

Nearly every night, he sat on the edge of my bed to tell me a bedtime story. My favorites all began with, "Many moons ago, there lived an Indian princess named Minnehaha." Back then I wanted to be Minnehaha because Dad spoke her name with such awe and tenderness.

If the weather allowed, Dad walked me to school every morning through sixth grade. During our commute, Dad explained things like why I didn't need a boyfriend in grade school, or why I shouldn't want to be a cheerleader: "Their skirts are far too short!" The week he taught me B.F. Skinner's theory of operant conditioning, he said, "Why don't we try it out, Honey Pot, on you?" And he conditioned me to pee when he whistled outside the bathroom. It was a useful trick at bedtime, one I taught my own children. And Chad.

Dad told me stories about living through the Depression, and explained how Morse code worked. After he waved goodbye at the gate of my school, he continued on to the college campus where he taught, three miles away.

Each weekday, Dad returned home around supper time, but then shortly after we ate, he'd disappear downstairs. In a corner of the basement, he set up a makeshift desk, where he arranged all of his telegrapher's gear. This corner he called his ham radio shack. There he passed the evening hours, sending and receiving messages from all over the world.

Often I climbed onto Dad's lap to watch him work. He slowly rotated the dial of the receiver, stopping when a signal sounded unusually strong. He transferred the headphones from his ears to mine so I could hear the cacophony of various voices and languages and the taps of telegraphers' keys communicating over hundreds and thousands of miles—dot dot dot dot, dash, dash ... Every time I promised to learn Morse code someday, Dad beamed.

Mom resented Dad's hobby and the long hours he spent downstairs. In the basement beneath his headset, he was oblivious to my brothers and me—our arguments and fistfights, our pranks on her.

Mom often threatened us with exclamations of, "Wait till your father gets off his radio!" But when she apprised Dad of our shenanigans—hiding tiny explosives in her cigarettes, or drinking all her Tab then filling up the bottle with water and food coloring—the punishment was rarely more than a guttural, "Run around the perimeter of the house three times, you rapscallions!"

Each night, Dad would climb the basement steps to re-enter our world just in time for the 11 o'clock news. He settled into his chair with a small dish of Spanish peanuts, the kind with greasy, papery red husks. He didn't mind that the husks made for a tooth-flossing nightmare. He didn't care much about personal hygiene except for combing his hair and beard. Because he rarely used deodorant, a single can of spray antiperspirant lasted him years.

To accompany his peanuts, Dad drank Pabst Blue Ribbon beer from a juice glass. He taught me to tilt the glass whenever I poured his beer so there wouldn't be much foam. Often, I feigned interest in the nightly news in hopes he'd offer me a peanut or a sip of beer before shooing me off to bed. Dad only let me dip my pinkie in the foam because he didn't want me to start drinking before I was eighteen.

CHAPTER FIFTEEN
The Secret Lives of Mom & Dad

Through the years I've pondered why our father never told us kids about Mom's mental illness. Perhaps at some point, Mom made Dad promise to stay silent about her dreadful diagnosis. And he did.

Or was Dad unconsciously mirroring Mom? My mother was mortified by her psychiatric condition. So much so she did her best to conceal it in all situations. Did Dad simply start to reflect his wife's secretive behavior?

In later years when it fell on me to accompany Mom to doctor's appointments, whenever caregivers asked for her medical history, Mom lied. At every appointment she acted as if her life was hunky-dory. She didn't peep about her psychiatric prescriptions either. Across the room, I'd make bug eyes, and she'd cut me with hers.

One time, as a nurse jotted down Mom's height and weight, I quickly whispered, without moving my lips, "She probably won't mention it, but my mom has depression." Another time, when Mom's doctor left the exam room, I told Mom I needed to go to the restroom. Instead, I found her physician in the hall and gave him a piece of key information: That week Mom had told me she'd been hearing voices. "Like a man on a microphone in a stadium."

If Mom knew I'd shared her secrets, she would've been livid. Every time I insisted, "Mom, the doctors and nurses can't help you if they don't know everything you're dealing with," she assured me they didn't need to know every little thing.

Was it possible Mom's disdain for this core part of herself eventually rubbed off on Dad? And my brothers. And me. Of all of us, I tended to be the hardest on my mother. Maybe part of me believed that if Mom had been healthy in every way, she would've protected me better. But since the majority of her energy went to keeping her mask in place—her facade of full function—not much was left for me.

Dad's silence may have been tied to his family. Did he feel he couldn't share Mom's difficulties with them because they were prosperous and quite proper? Dad's father worked as a banker, and later served as the state banking commissioner for a time. Dad's mother, Granny, was a strong and stylish matriarch. Granny insisted all five of her sons be born at home and informed my grandfather, "You will be present at every birth."

The recollection of that story made me think maybe Grandad was a seldom-seen father as well. Working long hours at the bank—or the state capitol—he left Granny to wrangle five boys, including one who was mentally ill and another who was legally blind.

According to Mom, Granny found fault with all of her daughters-in-law. With Mom, Granny criticized her lineage. How could the daughter of an Irish immigrant be good enough for her son Paul? Did Dad keep Mom's mental struggles to himself so as not to give Granny another reason to find fault with her?

Every time we visited Granny and Grandad, they required us to line up like the von Trapp children in *The Sound of Music*. After we finished Granny's enormous and delicious meal in the formal dining room, Grandad—in a suit, tie, and shiny Oxford shoes—held court in the living room. There he demanded reports of our academic progress and asked how much each of us weighed. He'd pull me onto his lap for a hug, where I'd wince at his halitosis and whisker-rough face.

After our "inspection," the four of us kids would scamper up the three flights of stairs to the attic to peruse the treasure trove of family memorabilia. Military uniforms, swords and pistols, fur coats, stacks of books, boxes of canned beans and Estée Lauder night cream, silver tea services, and colorful hand-stitched quilts.

Dad may have felt the need to conceal Mom's condition from his coworkers in the psychology department so they wouldn't consider him a psychological failure. In his own home. He was, after all, a psychology professor.

In his defense, the first degree Dad earned was in philosophy. Dad only pursued a master's degree in psychology—from Harvard on the G.I. Bill after World War II—because a nearby college needed a psychology professor. They hired him on the condition he'd earn a degree in psychology in the near future. Which he did. Years later, he also earned a PhD in psychometrics from Ohio State University. Probably because my father loved to learn. Or perhaps his parents urged him to—for the increase in salary and prestige. They were fond of both.

Since Dad specialized in psychometrics—psychological testing—not counseling or therapy, maybe he wasn't fully equipped to deal with Mom's issues. Or the rowdiness of us kids.

The four of us battled daily for the best breakfast cereal, for what show to watch on the basement TV, to see who could burp the loudest or hit the hardest, and to find out who could play the biggest prank on Mom. Jude would terrorize Tom, who would in turn take his anger out on me.

Mom was too weak to truly pay attention to us kids—to work to defuse our mutual animosity—but why didn't Dad make an effort? Was he too exhausted from Mom's nocturnal war waging, from walking six miles a day to and from work, from hiding Mom's ill health from his family and coworkers? For some reason he chose to maintain the illusion of familial function instead of working to make it happen.

Mom had said she and Dad followed the advice of the child development guru of their day, Dr. Benjamin Spock. She told me Dr. Spock espoused a hands-off philosophy with regard to parenting. But when I Googled more information on the famous pediatrician, I found an article saying things like, Spock was against corporal punishment, and he believed children need to hear they are loved and special. It didn't seem to me that Mom and Dad had read Dr. Spock's book after all. Perhaps Mom just watched him on *The Merv Griffin Show*.

CHAPTER SIXTEEN
Tom Boy

FOR TWO WHOLE DECADES, MAYBE MORE, MY BROTHER TOM despised me. In fact, when an introduction was necessary between me and his friends, he never said, "This is my little sister." Instead he'd say, "Her? She's just a pain in my butt, that's all." Even so, I thought he was the coolest guy ever. He was so funny he could make a dead man laugh.

One time I stood outside his bedroom door, my face smooshed to the wall just out of sight while he practiced a comedy skit in the mirror. I peeked in and saw him flop a pillowcase on his head, then watched as he undulated and sang, "King Tut, Tut. Funky Tut, Tut." I stole another look, giggling into my hand as he shimmied and crowed. "I'm just one wild and crazy guy."

When he finished, I pounced through the doorway with a grin. "You're the funniest guy ever! For real! They're gonna love you in the high school talent show."

That earned me a beating. For being a spy.

I should've apologized for the whipping Tom received that night on account of me. I did kind of invade his privacy. I also owed him several apologies for all the times I told Dad he was mean to me, knowing he'd get the belt.

Daddy believed me without fail. For no other reason than I was the only daughter, the youngest child. Every single time, Dad's face would flush super red, especially his nose, and his icy blue eyes would get tiny. "How could you hurt her? She's just a little girl, for crying out loud."

Tom's gaze would search the shadows for me. Then he'd mouth two words. "Spoiled brat." That phrase was his favorite thing to throw at me, besides a fist.

Despite the enmity between us when we were growing up, Tom was my favorite brother. Even though he did try to kill me once. On the chocolate milk–colored sofa in the basement. After I told him no way he was taking a date to my ninth-grade prom. He was way too old—two years and three months my senior—and besides, it was my school dance, not his. Plus, did he not know what Tammy Carter did with Joey Price behind the Convenient Mart? Did he really want to go out with a girl like that?

A moment later Tom launched at me, hands all T-Rex clawed, his mouth full of metal braces gleaming through a froth. He crammed my head into the arm of the couch then choked me until I saw stars, then nothing.

"Mom," I yelled after I came to. "Tom tried to murder me. I blacked out. I'm serious."

Mom didn't answer. She was in the backyard picking zinnias and cherry tomatoes.

I think maybe Tom and I were like Dad and our cat, Ginger. Dad was forever grouching about what a nuisance she was. All the time honking into the handkerchief he kept in his front pants pocket.

"That blankety-blank cat is single-handedly making Benadryl rich," Dad would roar.

Whenever Ginger perched on the sill outside the living room window, I'd remove the screen and let her in. Not Dad. He talked to her real nice, so she thought, maybe—then schwing! He'd crank the window open super fast and she'd go flying into the yard with a yowl.

And when she sat by the front door, daintily grooming her pumpkin paws, Dad would stroll up to her and point to his Hush Puppy Oxford. "Here, kitty, kitty. Let me introduce you to the number nine shoe. I don't believe you all have met." Once again, Ginger went flying with a yowl.

Ginger loved Daddy anyway. Whenever he fell asleep in his Ethan Allen wing chair during the nightly news, she'd sashay back and forth beneath his hand. She wasn't stupid though. As soon as Dad woke up, Ginger would hole up under his chair, her twitching tail the only evidence of her presence.

Surely Dad liked Ginger a tiny bit, because more than once I saw him give her an empty tuna can to lick when he thought no one was looking.

The way I figured it, Ginger was just like me. She wanted to be around the person who liked her least. She was okay with getting one pat on the back for every hundred times she went flying with a yowl. It didn't make a lick of sense, but she didn't care and neither did I.

Years later Tom and I grew close once we began comparing experiences and learning how much we had in common. We were both voted Class Clown in high school. We worked at the same fast-food biscuit restaurant, though not at the same time. Both of us were tormented by Jude. In fact, Tom tried to kill him once too.

When Tom was in junior high, tired of Jude's daily beatings, he did some research on self-defense. He thumbed through the pages of a book about martial arts until he came to a chapter describing dangerous and deadly blows. There he found an option he thought he could master. The book said the technique, if correctly delivered, could stop an attacker. However, this option should only be used in dire circumstances as it could severely disable or kill a person. Tom practiced the move again and again—a closed-fist punch to the Adam's apple.

"One afternoon," Tom told me, "I was in the pre-beating stage with Jude, and something clicked. It was time to make my move. Instead of cowering, I stood up. His eyes got big and he started laughing. 'What? What, you little motherfucker? What are you going to do?' He closed his eyes for a split second and I punched."

Breathless, I asked what happened next.

"His eyes opened wider and he grabbed his throat. Then I got an epic beating that lasted forever. I left my body till it was over. Later I remembered how, in martial arts, you're not supposed to practice hitting the target. You have to picture hitting through the target and not stopping at any resistance. That was my mistake. Probably the reason he's still alive."

CHAPTER SEVENTEEN
Middle Child Syndrome or...

THROUGH THE YEARS TOM HAS TOLD ME APPALLING STORIES ABOUT my parents' behavior toward him. Some of the incidents have literally haunted him. I know this because he tells the stories again and again.

After Tom attempted to kill Jude with a throat punch, and Jude started beating him, Tom broke away and ran downstairs. He fell prostrate at Mom's feet in submission, begging her for help as Jude thundered down the steps after him.

There in the living room, Tom clutched the leg of the couch and tried to make himself smaller and smaller, even attempting to crawl under the couch. Jude's kicks and punches ended up shoving Tom's head against the couch's wooden leg. Mom did nothing. She kept smoking and reading while Tom sobbed on the floor.

Finally, Mom glanced up from the book she was reading, exhaled a plume of cigarette smoke, and mumbled, "You boys go outside with that."

How was this humanly possible? How was this humanely possible?

Over the years, my parents frequently conveyed their frustrations about Tom. Dad often wondered aloud, "Why is Tom such a sad sack?" And Mom bemoaned the fact that as an adult, Tom had moved all the way out to California, since she and Dad hated to fly. "Will we ever see him again?"

I may have been a "spoiled brat," but even I could recognize the pecking order of the family. Mark was the golden child because he was quiet and obedient, made good grades, and in time would be a doctor. Jude was … well, Jude was just Jude. Like Mark, I held a special spot because I was the youngest child and the only girl. But Tom … Tom was forever on the outside looking in. I honestly think Mrs. Mac may have been his only friend. I wanted to be his friend, but Tom was so incensed toward all of us family members, there was no way he'd let that happen.

Where the heck was I during all of this insanity? I know exactly where I was. Gone. Out of the nuthouse. Every single day, I kept busy from the time I awoke until the time I fell into my bed.

I'd go to friends' houses and stay for hours, playing house, playing board games, helping my friends' mothers make applesauce, and baking cookies. I'd take our dog on long walks through the woods.

In the summer, my neighborhood friends and I would ride our bikes to the nearby cemetery, with packed lunches in our bike baskets, and explore every single road from right after breakfast until right before supper.

In the church parking lot across the street from my house, my friends and I would stage pretend horse shows on our bikes. We also played kickball and wiffle ball in a yard with a high fence. When I got to high school and made the tennis team, my tennis friends—guys and girls—and I would drive to the tennis courts with nighttime lights where we'd play until eleven. Then we'd return home and hang out on the neighborhood corner yakking until our mothers called us in.

I never, or rarely, witnessed my parents' neglect of Tom because

I was always elsewhere. As outside and alien as I felt in our family, Tom was infinitely more outside, alone, and alien. He inhabited another galaxy.

In later years, as much as Mom whined for Tom to come visit, when he finally did after Dad's death, she treated him abysmally. Her refrigerator held no food to speak of. On the guest bed there were no sheets or bedclothes. Instead, dusty storage boxes covered the mattress.

When Tom took Mom out to eat, she paid more attention to the people at the other tables than him, and when he tried to update her on his life, she informed him, loud enough for the people nearby to hear, "You talk too much. You're just like your father!"

Not surprisingly, Tom experienced a digestive mishap later that night and called me to come fetch him.

Who were these people, my family members?

And yet my mother, who mistreated her youngest son countless times, wrote these words in a notebook I found after her death.

> *December 28, 2005*
>
> *I got a horrible letter from Tom, full of hate especially about childhood. He does not intend to ever come to West Virginia and will not accept visitors.*
>
> *I have lost a son. I will pray for him. I wish he could find someone that could help him to think straight and be sane. He just wants to be left alone. He hates me. I was a poor mother.*
>
> *I feel this way. Nothing is as bad as a parent losing a child before them. I will pray for him. For him to find someone to help him. I can leave him alone. He does hate me. He remembers every bad thing and doesn't remember any good things. So sad. I will not rate myself. I am just a fallible human being.*
>
> *I have no proof that Tom won't change. I believe God will*

help him. He has suffered so long. Family is praying for him. I have faith that he will be okay.

Again, who were these people?

On impulse one night, I Googled, "Do parents sometimes treat one child horribly but not the others?" Lo and behold, dozens, hundreds—the screen actually said there were millions—of results loaded in seconds.

Some articles pointed toward "middle child syndrome," where the middle kid gets ignored because they're not the oldest and not the youngest. One article said if a child is significantly different from the parents, they may be mistreated. One expert explained that many families have an "unfavored child." However, docile children, obedient children, and kids who are academically successful and polite usually find favor with their parents.

One article spoke of the dangers of "parental favoritism." The list of negative side effects and behavior for kids who are basically rejected is long. I see many of those side effects and behaviors in my brother Tom.

Tom ended one of his emails to me, after a not-unusual rant against the family, with two sentences. "I do not like or love my mother or father. I do not like or love either of my brothers." Frankly, I didn't blame him a bit.

Looking for clues one night, I created a massive document with emails from Tom. Many of his accounts turned my stomach, like this one.

> *"I'm trying hard to remember the age when Jude began to fondle me. I'm pretty sure it was before third grade, whatever age that would make me. I specifically recall him being especially friendly to me, which I ate up, of course.*
>
> *"Then he gave me his grown-up magazine to look at. And*

he would get under the covers and start doing stuff. I remember telling him to stop, that I didn't like it because it would start to hurt after a bit. He would look wide-eyed and try to keep my attention on the magazine. It was like he was trying to make me enjoy something that I had no idea about, or interest in. He would do this and make promises, saying he'd do other things with me, play flashlight tag and such, to keep me hanging in there."

CHAPTER EIGHTEEN
Mark My Word

I LOVED MY BROTHER MARK, DEEPLY, BECAUSE HE WAS DIFFERENT, definitely something else, as the saying goes. His heart felt pure to me. Probably because he never came at me with stealth, a certain anarchy oozing from his pores. And not once did he approach me with hands choke-hold ready and cheeks stop-sign red. Mark was different. A low tide. Quiet, steady.

Whenever I passed by the bookshelf with Mark's senior portrait, eight inches by eleven inside an ornate fake-gold frame, I'd admire the way his hair did a swoosh like the bunny slope at Canaan Valley ski resort. A smooth, nut-brown arc with one perfect dip in the middle.

In his portrait, Mark's eyes seemed serious even as they smiled. Did he already know he had healing—and therefore much responsibility—in his hands? His irises matched the widest stripe in his chubby tie—blue-gray sky on a fall morning.

Mark and I dabbled in so many things, I made a list in one of my journals, so as not to forget a one of them. If memory serves, our first endeavor was hatha yoga. We'd both spread our campfire-fragranced sleeping bags on the cement basement floor and strike various poses, attempting to copy the elegance of public television's

Lilias in her leotard. Mark always envied my ability to get my knees to touch the ground in butterfly pose.

The two of us also lifted weights together. Or rather, Mark lifted weights and I watched. Because he'd read somewhere my bones wouldn't be ready for resistance work until at least fourth grade. Wanting to be exactly like my oldest brother, I wept, but Mark held firm.

After our resistance training phase, we moved on to archery. We set up a practice range behind the house by cramming a target into the tangle of honeysuckle that concealed the chain-link fence at the back of our yard. Skill-wise, he and I were evenly matched until our flimsy green bow broke and he replaced it with a red, white, and blue compound model. Since I couldn't budge the string to save my life, Mark appointed me the arrow fetcher.

Then during his freshman year of college, Mark professed faith in Jesus Christ as his Lord and Savior and worked hard to persuade me to do the same. Whenever he visited for a weekend, he'd invite me to accompany him to the church he attended across the river in Ohio. We'd hold our breath as we drove over the bridge, and if our breath held, we'd make a wish on other side. Mark thought we could get famous as a gospel group since I was taking piano lessons, but that idea petered out once he fell in love with a tiny coal miner's daughter. It was for the best, though. Mark's plaintive, off-pitch singing voice made my right eyelid twitch.

Mark and I also journeyed through France together via the Julia Child cooking show on public television. I still have her recipe for flaming crepes suzette. The velvety butter and orange sauce and the delicate crepes—Mark's steady hands were so good at flipping crepes without tearing them—tasted extraordinary, even though Mom wouldn't let us do the flaming part.

One of my favorite memories of Mark is when he was in osteopathic medical school. Whenever he came home for a visit, he'd practice doing osteopathic manipulations on me, cracking my back and tugging on my arms and legs to stretch them. "You'd make a way better doctor than me," Mark said one time. When I snorted, he said, "No, really. You're way smarter than me." I loved hearing that, because Mark was pretty darn smart.

Mark never told me outright that he enjoyed spending time with me, but he didn't have to. All the stuff we did together showed it, proved that he was in fact something else, something better than favorite. I might go as far as to say he was the best brother.

CHAPTER NINETEEN
All About Jude

WHERE MARK MAY HAVE BEEN MY BEST BROTHER AND TOM MY funniest, Jude was my strongest brother, in more ways than one. Actually he was the strongest person in our entire family. Or perhaps *powerful* would be a more appropriate word to use. I believe every person in our family feared Jude for one reason or another.

In old family photos, Jude is the cutest of us kids. In time, he grew up to be quite handsome in a lean and tawny, leonine way. In youth, his curls were copper-colored and his eyes swimming pool blue.

Believing it enhanced his desirability, Jude sported a deep bronze tan. To that end, he would lie out in the backyard, often with me and Katie Lynn, who resembled a cross between Cher and Brooke Shields. Afterward, sweaty and slick with Hawaiian Tropic dark tanning oil, Jude opted not to shower. The next day he'd repeat the process. And the next. Jude held a theory that the accumulated dirt would further deepen his tan. Miraculously, he never smelled bad.

My other memories of Jude are random. The way Mom and Dad never figured out he was growing pot in his room. To smoke the weed he cultivated, Jude jerry-rigged a pipe out of a salt shaker shaped like a catfish. He'd get high up in his room too, but our parents never noticed that either.

When my beginner bras—stretchy and lacy, but far from substantial—went missing multiple times, along with my prettier pairs of underpants, I blamed Jude. Because of his nighttime behavior. He would deny the thievery, though, when I accused him, saying, "Now why would I want to do that? You're fat and flat."

After Mom taught me the basics of driving a car, she instructed Jude to take me driving weekly to get more practice. I was terrified he might attempt in the car in broad daylight what he did in our house in darkness. Thankfully he never did, but always those outings petrified me.

In our family's lime sherbet–colored Buick Skylark, Jude would drive me down to the boat docks and park, then shoo me behind the wheel. "Your turn."

Jude's choice of a practice location concerned me. For starters, the downtown boat dock was much farther from home than the graveyard where Mom, and sometimes Dad, took me driving. And then there was the presence of the wide and swiftly flowing Ohio River right next to the parking lot. There was an opening in the protective floodwall where drivers of station wagons and pickup trucks could ease canoes and pleasure boats into the water.

Jude enjoyed directing me to drive toward the water until the last moment, when he'd command me to steer into a swooping turn away from it. One evening my reflexes weren't fast enough, and both of the car's front tires dipped into the Ohio River and spun a little. I slammed the car into park as my eyes filled with hot panicked tears. "Were you not even going to tell me to stop?" I shrieked. I wasn't sure I'd survive driving lessons with Jude.

In the winter, because Dad thought it would be prudent for me to know how to drive in the snow, he sent Jude and me out every weekend. Since Jude loved to drive in the snow, he almost always ended up driving more than me during our lessons. He would transport us to some expansive, snow-blanketed parking lot where he could show me a new skill. Donuts.

I'd hold my breath and death-grip my lap safety belt with both hands while Jude accelerated the car to his preferred speed. Fast. Then he'd stomp on the brake pedal while turning the steering wheel hand over hand as hard as he could to the left, causing our car to slide into multiple circular spins until it kind of shuddered to a stop. A moment later, to make sure he covered all the bases of proper instruction, Jude repeated the maneuver, this time, whipping the steering wheel to the right.

Part of me liked doing donuts with Jude. Most of me didn't. During this activity, he often howled like a madman. Between his howls and the stomach-wrenching car twirls, I felt a little crazy too.

Then there was the time Jude and a buddy snuck a case of Rolling Rock beer into our basement. Katie Lynn was spending the night, and when she and I went downstairs to watch TV, there they were: the boys and the beer.

"Want some?" Jude asked.

I said no. Katie Lynn said yes.

As we drained four, then eight bottles of beer, we could hear the drone of the television in the living room above us, the sporadic murmur of my parents' conversation. Though the green Rolling Rock bottles were pretty, I disliked the beer's bitter taste. I hoped Dad would come downstairs and discover us being bad so I wouldn't have to drink any more. Plus, if my father found us drinking, no doubt he'd give Jude the belt for corrupting me and Katie Lynn.

But that night in the basement Jude sat alert, facing the steps, ready to head off a confrontation. Every time I raised my voice in raucous laughter, Jude flashed his you're-going-to-get-us-in-trouble look. No one ever checked on us that night. No one figured out two college boys were getting two ninth-grade girls tipsy in the basement.

The next day, I decided not to tell Dad about the incident. Even though I didn't care for the taste of beer, I sure did like the way it turned up my giddy and tamped down my mad.

Only one time did I ride on Jude's motorcycle with him. He wore nothing but a helmet, cut-off jean shorts, and old sneakers. At an alarming speed, he took me on a twisty road. Rounding a curve, he leaned the bike so close to the road I thought surely we would die.

Jude followed up that trick with an extended wheelie. I waited for us to tip over backward as we covered a considerable distance on his rear tire only. From that day forward I refused to go anywhere with Jude on his motorcycle.

Jude drove me to a secret swimming hole once. A number of his friends were there, and there was beer and maybe pot. With icy water gushing down from higher altitudes, I was scared to swing from, then let go of, the high-up rope swing. How deep was the water? How fast was the current? Were there boulders below the surface? But Jude made me. He wouldn't let me say no.

Jude didn't excel in school, team sports, or music. However, later in life, he became skilled at skiing, snowboarding, and cycling. While living at home, though, the only thing he excelled in was partying. Beer, pot, magic mushrooms, you name it, Jude would try anything. In fact, one of his friends joked to me once that Jude was a try-sexual. "He'll try anything once." And anybody, I added inside my mind.

The only pastime I remember Jude having besides getting a buzz was hobby rockets. All three of my brothers loved assembling and launching them. Every time they trekked to the nearby graveyard to set off rockets, I'd follow close behind.

I hated the times when the boys squeezed a mouse from the pet store into the body tube along with the fuel cartridges. It was Jude's idea to see if the mice would survive a trip to outer space. They never did.

My one good memory of Jude involved his part-time job at McDonald's. After his training, it didn't take Jude long to notice that when prepared foods weren't purchased within five minutes, management would throw them away. So for months, Jude intentionally made too much food in the minutes before his shift ended so he could bring home bags of burgers, fries, apple pies, and milkshakes. On those occasions, I actually thought Jude was pretty cool.

CHAPTER TWENTY
The Big (to me) Macs

IN SUMMER WHEN THE HEAT AND HUMIDITY SOARED, WE CRANKED the windows wide. In each room, a beige box fan hummed. When Mom shrieked like an obnoxious fishwife, I despaired that our neighbors might be shocked by the noise. Then I remembered what Mom said on a regular basis. Everyone on our street had air-conditioning except us. With their windows closed and their cooling units purring, they couldn't hear a thing—not the crickets, not the neighborhood cats caterwauling, and not Mom. Lucky them.

But what about Mr. and Mrs. McCallister next door? Could they hear? They had central air, but hated to close up their house, so they rarely used it. Next to their spacious white Cape Cod with forest-green shutters, our brick house appeared puny. Their backyard was huge, easily twice the size of ours. Mr. McCallister gave me permission to play there whenever I wanted, which was almost daily. I adored the sprawling magnolia tree in the center of their lawn, with its glossy dark leaves and humongous creamy blossoms that broadcast summer's perfume throughout the neighborhood. I loved creasing the waxy petals to watch the lines brown.

The neighborhood kids called the McCallisters Mr. and Mrs.

Mac. Mom called Mrs. Mac "Dainty" because she was so tiny, I guess. My nickname for her would be "Sunny" because she was always warm and in a good mood. If she didn't sleep with her hair wound around prickly curlers, she resembled a scarecrow topped with a stainless-steel scrubbing pad. Her eyes were the color of dried cornflowers on the roadside, with a gray-brown tint of gravel dust. Whenever she and I ventured out to her backyard to flick ants off her peony plants, if the sun was right, I could almost see through her.

Mrs. Mac was like a bonus grandmother to me. I always ran to her house when things got heated at mine. Like the day Jude slammed his fist through a wall upstairs.

"Come in, dear," Mrs. Mac said, cracking the screen door. "Things rough at home? You hungry?" I always said yes, even if I wasn't. It made her happy to spoil me. It made me happy to be spoiled.

Aware of my powerful sweet tooth, Mrs. Mac frequently offered me strawberry rhubarb pie or bowls heaped high with lemon ice cream. Or tapioca pudding. Even though the little spheres reminded me of fish eyeballs, I loved the vanilla sweetness of the dish.

Sometimes she served me buttermilk sprinkled with salt and pepper. One day she convinced me to try stewed tomatoes over torn-up white bread. I didn't think I'd care for it, but I ended up asking for seconds, then thirds.

My very favorite thing to eat in Mrs. Mac's kitchen, with its brick-looking linoleum floor, was wilted lettuce with tiny green onion hoops doused with bacon-grease dressing. The dense cloud of congealed fat in a Maxwell House coffee can on her counter grossed me out, but when Mrs. Mac melted a lump of it in her cast-iron skillet and splashed it with cider vinegar, it tasted wonderful, tangy. Especially on leaf lettuce that had been torn from her garden that morning.

During the summer, she and I watched Phil Donahue on her black-and-white TV. Each morning before Donahue began, I stretched out on one of the two pine-green Naugahyde chaise lounges in the Macs' sitting room. Mrs. Mac carried her blue parakeet, Dickey Bird, on her pointer finger and coaxed him to perch on my shoulder. "You tell him everything, dear. Talk to him as long as you want, long as you need." She always moved away before I could say I'd rather talk to her than Dickey Bird.

After Donahue ended, she often asked if I wanted to see her dolls. I didn't want to say yes, but I usually did, to please her. Upstairs in the guest bedroom, we inspected her dozens of prize-winning porcelain babies, all of them in ridiculous frilly dresses.

I didn't play with dolls much. Dolls were for girls who wanted to be mommies. I had no desire to be a mother when I grew up. The only person I wanted to care for was me. I rarely accepted babysitting jobs because I had no idea what to do with babies. Instead, I ran an afternoon paper route. I took over Mark's when he left for college. Passing papers, even in inclement weather, was way better than wiping baby butts and noses.

I wasn't sure I wanted to get married, either. Marriage meant needing someone. It also meant telling someone how you feel, and I was like my dad—I'd rather not. Plus, I'd have to pretend I liked doing the things people did when they were naked. I already knew I didn't.

I'm pretty sure Mrs. Mac knew what was going on at our house because years later, Tom told me she'd suggested he take a baseball bat to Jude. When Tom said that, I knew he'd told her Jude was doing more than just beating him daily. Jude was doing to Tom the same kind of stuff he was doing to me. Part of me wanted details, part of me didn't. Though I hated what Jude did to me, it seemed more normal than what he was doing to Tom—another boy. I was jealous that Tom confided in Mrs. Mac. I suffered my shame alone.

Where my secret made me pissy, Tom's filled him with fury. One night when Mom, Dad, and I came home from eating out, we found deep gashes in all the wood furniture on the first floor. Tom was the only one home.

CHAPTER TWENTY-ONE
The Boy Bedroom

IN BETWEEN OUR LIVING ROOM AND DINING ROOM WAS A SET OF stairs that led up to the second floor and its three rooms: the boy bedroom, a bathroom, and Dad's office.

Both upstairs rooms had plywood doors, stained a honey color, that led to attic storage spaces. The attic in the boy bedroom was filled with boxes of photo albums and out-of-season clothes. The attic in the other room held crates of Dad's vinyl albums, mostly classical music.

I can't remember if I ever envied the boys all sleeping together in one room. Probably not, since from early on I knew what Jude was capable of. To have him sleeping a few feet away from me would have been ghastly.

Tom's twin bed snuggled the left wall, and had a military trunk near the footboard. Tom used the trunk as a hobby table. He loved to paint toy soldiers and build plastic models of army vehicles. He proudly displayed them at the foot of his bed. Like my various undergarments, Tom's creations often went missing. He found more than one plastic military vehicle in the woods, almost unrecognizable in the center of a cold campfire site.

The quilt on Tom's bed was red, white, and blue, with illustrated scenes from the Revolutionary War. Tom loved war stuff. Just like Dad.

Mark and Jude slept together in a full-sized bed positioned in the center of the back wall. Their bed was covered in a scarlet corduroy comforter backed with a soft paisley fabric. A couple of dressers and a desk filled the remainder of the wall space.

I remember countless games of Tickle Monster on that bed. One person, the designated Tickle Monster, would hide under the covers, grabbing and groping at any body part he or she could get a hold of. The goal was for the Tickle Monster to take someone down. When that happened, the fallen individual became the Tickle Monster.

Sometimes the tickling took place with all of us on top of the corduroy comforter. Other times the four of us would wage a tickle war on the floor. On several occasions all three of my brothers held me down and tickled me for what seemed like forever. "Laugh! Laugh!" they'd bellow. Never once did I laugh. Not one time did I giggle. I refused to give my brothers any satisfaction for what felt to me like torture. Plus, by then I was a pro at staying silent and not moving a muscle. To this day, I can't stand being tickled.

Tom told me the story of begging Dad to let him sleep with the big boys in their bed one night. After much cajoling, Dad agreed that Tom could sleep in the older boys' bed in between them. Tom ended up quietly crying himself to sleep that night as both brothers kicked and punched at him in the dark. Tom kept quiet, though, not wanting to be sent back to his own bed.

I remember afternoons in the summertime when Mom and I would sit in the living room, both of us with our noses in books. When it sounded like thunder was rumbling, she and I would glance up at the ceiling—the boy bedroom was over the living room—waiting to see if it would fall down on us. This was the boys "raising Cain," as Mom and Dad called it.

When the noise grew particularly rowdy, Mom sent me upstairs to spy. I'd army crawl up the steps—silently, of course—and peek into the boy bedroom. Usually, my brothers were simply chasing each other around the spacious room, slipping and sliding in stocking feet on the hardwood floors and taking wild swings at one another.

But every now and then, my report to Mom would cause her to set down her book and light a cigarette, shaking her head as she did so. "Call your father. Tell him he needs to come home. Right now." Like the time Jude punched through the wall into the attic area. Being a registered nurse, Mom thought his bloody hand might need medical attention.

I phoned Dad's office, but didn't get to talk to him. I rarely did. Almost always, his elegant elderly secretary took a message. "I'll see if I can get him to call you back, honey, but right now he's teaching class."

I thanked her, hung up, and tiptoed across the kitchen floor to the door that led to our tiny side porch. Without telling Mom, I nudged open the door without a noise, darted down the steps to the yard, then sprinted up the hill to Mrs. Mac's house.

On the Macs' porch, I made goggles of my hands to peer through their screen door into the shadows of their sitting room. Dainty was lying on her sofa, eyes closed, her body so still I thought for a moment she might be dead.

I pecked lightly on the screen door. If she didn't wake up, I'd leave. But I prayed she would indeed wake up. I needed a safer place to be at the moment, a place that didn't throb with boy energy, especially Jude's. Mrs. Mac's eyes fluttered open when Dickey Bird started chirping, "Hello! Dickey Bird! Hello!"

Possibly the first time my parents became fully aware that something was seriously wrong with us kids came when Mark refused to ever sleep in the boy bedroom again. No one knew why.

He was maybe fifteen.

According to Mom, Mark was having issues. In Mom's words, "Mark just clammed up. He wouldn't hardly talk about anything to anyone." Mark was so upset, he slept in the hall, squeezed between a bookshelf and a rocking chair, until my parents prepared a room for him.

Mom said at that point she and Dad had no idea what Jude was up to because Tom had not yet come forward. Tom didn't disclose his abuse by Jude until he graduated from college and left the state in 1983.

Not knowing how to loosen Mark's lips, Dad asked another psychology professor to come to our home and talk to Mark. But Mark gave no explanation to Dad's coworker either. He wouldn't utter a word. His face was pale, as if he was in shock.

After that, Mom and Dad gave up. They didn't try any other strategies to solve the Mark mystery. Why didn't they get him counseling? I wondered. Mom got lots of therapy. Maybe she and Dad discussed it, but never in my presence.

I asked Mom at one point if she and Dad ever recognized that something was wrong with Jude. Since he was so wild, he was a difficult kid to parent. I wish I'd kept up that line of questioning. Instead, I changed the subject, asking Mom if she thought Jude had threatened Mark to keep him quiet. Immediately, she nodded her head in agreement. "Yes!"

I remembered seeing the hole in the boy bedroom wall. And Jude's damaged hand bleeding. I recalled being alone in the car with him, not knowing what he might do next. That feeling could shut you up for a good long time.

What could possibly have happened to cause Mark to exit the boy bedroom? Did Jude do unspeakable things to Mark, or at least try? Or did he witness Jude doing those things to Tom? It was one of those two possibilities. I was sure of it.

I always said, ever since the fourth grade, I knew I'd get counseling and I knew I'd write a book. I was in fourth grade the year Mark moved out of the boy bedroom.

CHAPTER TWENTY-TWO
Looking Back

After Mark moved out of the boy bedroom, what all did Tom endure in the years before Jude left for college? Maybe a whole lot, perhaps not much. On at least one occasion, Tom hypothesized that at some point in time, he believed Jude had transferred his attention to me.

It made me wonder how our psychology professor father had failed to recognize that two of his kids, maybe three, were being sexually abused by the fourth one? I wanted to know if my parents ever actually confronted Jude regarding my accusation. Did Dad really accost Jude on my behalf? If so, I wasn't around when it happened.

Jude never apologized to me. I didn't get sent to counseling, and neither did Jude. It was yet another opportunity missed. I know now that the majority of sibling sexual offenders who receive proper treatment never abuse anyone again.

So much relational rubble, but our family plodded on intact with no investigation or intervention whatsoever. No one kicked Jude out of our family. Except for me. I shunned him for years. Until I didn't. I broke my silence with him because he told me he was sorry. For everything.

For a period of time, Jude won. Mom and Dad didn't disinherit him. Mark never stopped being a brother to him, and I was on speaking terms with him again.

The person who ended up on the outside—the biggest loser—was Tom. He married a woman who in time revealed herself to be a troublesome human with secrets of her own. Six, actually. She mailed much of the money she and Tom earned to her six children, whom Tom knew nothing about, in another country. Plus she verbally abused him every month when her cycle came calling.

Eventually Tom ghosted her. One day while she worked, he moved all his belongings elsewhere, and their marriage was done. For the next decade or two, Tom lived alone on the West Coast, far from West Virginia, far from Mom and Dad, who had failed him, and far from me, the "spoiled brat."

Multiple times Chad and I urged Tom to get counseling.

"For what?" he always asked.

"For a difficult childhood, a terrible marriage."

"Why bother?" he responded. "Whatever Jude did to me is over and done with."

So many men refuse help for child sexual abuse. Ashamed they weren't strong enough to prevent or stop the abuse, they can't crawl out from beneath the weighty stone of shame that crushes them. This is all the more difficult if their abuser was also male, which is usually the case.

This was a tragedy in Tom's life. He was so funny, I believed he could've enjoyed a career in stand-up comedy. He was very bright, and a spiffy dresser too. I loved his huge heart for animals. We both inherited that from Mom.

I once created a social media image that said, "Dear survivor: If you stay silent, they win." Tom was, for the most part, silent about his abuse. Which meant Jude won. With Tom, at least.

Not with me, though. I will not stay silent so Jude can stay comfortable. Instead, I will do the very thing Mom deemed unforgivable. I will "air our family's dirty laundry." I will open our family's closet and let the multitudinous skeletons tumble out with a clatter.

PART THREE

The Waiting
2002–2005

CHAPTER TWENTY-THREE
Decline

In the summer of 2002, Dad's health was continuing to deteriorate. Concerned for Mom, I called my brother Mark and read from the latest Alzheimer's Association newsletter I'd received: "The primary caregiver, be it a spouse, child, or paid professional, needs a break on a regular basis. Otherwise, there is a risk of caregiver burnout."

Mark agreed that Mom needed help at home, so I offered to do the research since I lived closer. Later that day, I flipped through the phone book searching for home health agencies near Mom and Dad. I spotted a small display ad for "Home Health Angels." Angels, I thought, that's sweet.

I spoke with Ron, the manager, about Mom and Dad's status and the Angels' services and rates.

When I relayed the information to Mom, she was all for it. "With someone else looking after Paul, maybe I can go to Myrtle Beach."

The first three days with a hired caregiver went well. Then the agency sent over someone new, a young girl named Amanda. Mom liked her. Dad did not. After they took him away, Mom called me.

Amanda had been curling Mom's hair when Dad confronted her.

Who was she and why was she in his house? The girl smiled and explained who she was. When she paused, Dad slapped her and she went down. With raised fists, he glared at her. Mom told Amanda to run. Within an hour, an ambulance transported Dad to the psychiatric ward of the local hospital. My daddy, my smart daddy.

Early the next week, Mom phoned to say she'd found a personal care home for Dad. The facility was basically a rambling older home with a small staff that cared for the elderly residents, who each rented a bedroom. When I reminded Mom the plan was to move Dad to a nursing home, she assured me this place was homier. I rolled my eyes. You mean, cheaper, I thought.

I told her what I'd read in the Alzheimer's Association newsletter: "Every move and change in routine accelerates the mental decline of the person with dementia."

Later that week Mom called to inform me Dad was once again in the psych ward. The personal care home evicted him because he wouldn't keep his clothes on. As Mom spoke, I stretched out on the sofa, my forearm covering my eyes.

"At least he's on the list now," Mom said.

I uncovered my eyes. "What list?"

"The nursing home list, but he can't be moved until a bed opens up, and a bed won't open up until—"

"Until when?"

Her voice was hushed. "Until someone dies."

"This stinks," I growled.

"I hope a bed becomes available at the senior community over here by me. They have a five-star chef."

The next time Mom and I spoke, she had news. A bed was available in a nearby nursing home. In a matter of days, Dad could be transported to the facility in Kingmont. The fact that Kingmont was halfway between her house and ours thrilled me, but not Mom. She reiterated that she wanted Dad in the senior living community near her. In fact, she planned to move him there as soon as—

"Don't you get it, Mom? Every move makes him worse. No more moves!"

"We'll see."

When we visited Providence Manor for the first time, Chad and I didn't take the kids. As I sat across from Dad, I fought to keep from crying. He was motionless, and his skin was so pale, he seemed made of wax. His head lolled forward as if it was too heavy to hold up.

I whispered to Chad. "How did he get so bad so fast?"

Chad said it was probably all the changes Dad had been through. On my fingers, I counted Dad's recent relocations. Five.

"He'll never smile again. What do you want to bet?" I paced in front of Dad's geri chair. "Look at him. He's wretched. Pitiful."

Chad frowned as he studied my father's empty expression.

I rattled Dad's tray. It was locked tight to his wheelchair. "Look at this contraption. It's a prison on wheels. He'll probably never walk again either."

Chad raised his pointer finger to his lips. "He can still hear, you know."

"Hear what? Blah, blah, blah! That's all he hears now. What good is a PhD when you can't walk or talk? When you don't even know your own daughter?" I gripped the sides of Dad's tray. "Who am I, Dad? Say my name."

Dad didn't move, or even blink. Instead he mumbled and drew circles on his tray. A moment later I pressed on his hands to still his fingers. "Why didn't I ever learn Morse code like I promised? If I had, you and I could be communicating right now. I'm sure of it."

After five minutes of studying what my father had become, I suddenly grabbed the sides of his large pink bib and yanked.

When the Velcro gave way, Chad gasped. "Good night, Dina!"

"No bib! No father of mine, and certainly not one with a degree from Harvard, is going to wear a stupid, stinking bib."

Chad hooked his hand under my arm and tugged. "Come on. Let's go. We'll come back next Sunday. Maybe he'll be better then."

After our initial visit, Chad, the kids, and I did our best to spend at least one Sunday a month with Dad. We wheeled him into the sunny dining room where I played the piano, Sophia the flute, and Lark the violin. Occasionally, Dad hummed along to the music. One time, he swooped his hands like a conductor. Another time, when we played "Amazing Grace," Dad immediately started singing along. Even if it was only for a moment, our music rescued him from wherever he'd gone.

During our visits, Wyatt kept Dad's tray stocked with snacks. Usually I brought a cheeseburger kid's meal and a candy bar to assuage Dad's well-known hankering for sweet and salty foods. His arm and fingers operated like a crane to relocate the pieces of food from the tray to his tongue—pinch, lift, swing, release. He grunted with satisfaction as a viscous stream of chocolate or French fry drool made its way to his beard.

Each time we visited, my father seemed a little less himself. After we played music, I sat across from him and took inventory of his appearance. I held one-sided conversations with him, pretending he understood me. "Oh, Daddy, you lost a tooth, and it's one of the ones in front." I blinked back tears. "Oh, Pops, who shaved off your beard? You don't resemble Abraham Lincoln anymore."

I smiled as I remembered the day Mom and I begged Dad to shave off his beard and mustache. He did it in stages—from bushy beard down on the neck to neat and trimmed beard along the jaw. Beneath his nose, his thick, full mustache became a Hitler-hyphen.

As soon as he was clean-shaven, Mom and I were dismayed. "Quick, grow it back! You don't have a chin."

When I told Chad the story, he chuckled and slid his fingertips across Dad's cheek. "I like your dad without a beard. He has a nice face."

Every time we visited, Dad drew circles on his tray and muttered the same phrases over and over: "The men climbed on the trains, the trains carried the men to the boats, and the boats took the men out to the islands."

Dad was describing the war, I told Chad. In World War II, Dad served as a telegrapher in the Navy. When I was younger, he'd told me how at seventeen, he'd lied about his age to enlist. Any job would be better than being a boring banker like his father.

Some days I read Bible stories to Dad. I wondered if he remembered the church across the street from our house, and how Mom and I sat on his right and Mark, Jude, and Tom sat on his left. While the pastor preached, Tom drew pictures of military equipment, and I sketched pictures of Secretariat with the garland of roses he won in the Kentucky Derby. My brothers tried to outsing Dad and me on hymns like "Morning Has Broken" and "This Is My Father's World."

Sometimes I asked Dad if Granny ever took him to church when he was small. Instead of answering, he traced more circles. "And the men climbed on the trains ..."

In the spring of 2002, roughly six months before Dad completely lost his mind, I had been baptized. Mark and his wife, Valerie, attended, as well as my friend Bobbi. An older woman and an eight-year-old boy went in the water with me. In the hotel swimming pool, before our pastor waded in to join us, I confided to my baptism buddies that I felt like I was marrying Jesus.

"I heard you got baptized," Dad had said the next time we visited him and Mom. His pale blue eyes seemed brighter, more lucid than I'd seen in months. It was as if a fire burned somewhere inside of him, and its glow flickered in his eyes. "Congratulations,

Dina Sue! I just know your Granny was watching from heaven saying, 'Bless you, honey child, bless you.'"

As Dad's eyes misted over, I held my breath. To have those tears and say those words, surely my father possessed faith. I wanted him to have faith, so I'd see him again someday. He left my side and strode across the room to lean against the mantle. From there he told us a story about when his mother, my Granny, was young. "She was a wee slip of a thing. Like her," he said, pointing to Lark who grinned up at him. All three kids sat cross-legged on the floor by the sofa, spellbound by their Doc's story. Doc was their nickname for him.

"The ladies in her neighborhood took turns bringing her to church. She loved the hymns." Dad cleared his throat and launched into one. "I come to the garden alone—" When the kids applauded, Dad bowed slightly. He told us how Granny had loved Bible stories —Noah and the ark, David and Goliath, Jonah and the whale.

In front of the television, Dad blocked Mom's view of The Weather Channel. "One day, Granny asked the neighborhood ladies, 'May I please be baptized?' They said, 'If it's all right with your folks, wear a white dress to church next Sunday.' When Granny asked her parents, they said it was fine with them. She didn't own a white dress so she brought a nightgown and wore it over her dress when they dunked her in the crick that runs alongside Simpson Creek Baptist Church. It was a chilly day, but she didn't mind. She said it was like she was marrying Jesus."

Prickles ran the length of my back.

Then just like that, the light in Dad's eyes departed. He sank down on the sofa and stared out the bay window. As I studied his profile, I marveled at the five or ten minutes when he reminded me of a prophet—Moses or Elijah, maybe—electric with the spirit.

"What about you, Dad? Did you ever get baptized?"

My father didn't answer. He didn't say another word that day.

Even though Dad knew hymns and could name a few Bible stories, Mom had informed me years ago that she and Dad didn't believe in hell. I figured if they didn't believe in hell, they probably didn't believe the rest of the Bible either. When I mentioned that to Mom, she didn't argue.

"Why bother going to church then?"

Mom had flipped her counted cross-stitch project over and snipped a thread. "It's a good place to meet people and make friends."

I studied Dad on the plaid sofa, all tuckered out from storytelling. His account of Granny's baptism made me feel closer to her and him. I wondered if her belief ever transferred to any of her five sons. Dad never exhibited any kind of commitment to religion other than his insistence that we kids attend either church or Sunday school every week.

Now that his rational mind was ebbing away, maybe a new spiritual one had replaced it. Or perhaps a faith, from when he was a little boy with flaxen hair, had been called forth. Is that why he told the story of Granny's baptism? Was his deep calling out to mine?

That day was the last time my father ever spoke my name.

CHAPTER TWENTY-FOUR
Dire Diagnosis

THERE WAS A SHADOW IN MOM'S VOICE THE NEXT TIME SHE phoned. On the back porch, I lowered myself onto the top step and braced for the latest drama.

"Peg is dying."

I squinted at the forsythia bushes starting to burst forth in glorious bloom at the back of our yard. "What are you talking about?" She repeated her statement. I sagged. Not Peg.

Peg was my favorite aunt. She and Mom shared the same vivid blue eyes and high cheekbones. Her laugh sounded like a happy machine gun. I adored her bronze, lacquered beehive hair-do and her always-lipsticked smile.

"How do you know? Are you sure?"

Mom's voice wobbled as she told me Peg's abdomen was alarmingly distended. Mom believed that meant Peg had some sort of cancer.

"Wait. Has she not seen a doctor yet?"

"No, but her appointment is soon."

"If there's no diagnosis, why are you jumping the gun?"

And yet, Mom was right. The doctor diagnosed Aunt Peg with

ovarian cancer, late stage. Two days later, an oncologist scheduled her for surgery to remove the mass.

On the day of Aunt Peg's operation, I walked around our yard picking flowers to take her: daffodils, bleeding hearts, and grape hyacinths. Wrapping the stems in a damp paper towel, I secured them with a twist tie and tucked the bouquet into a baggie, the way Mom taught me when I was little.

At the hospital, I slipped into the chair next to my aunt's bed and watched as she opened her eyes and took a moment to recognize her all-white surroundings. Eventually she noticed me and managed a smile. The fingers of her right hand lifted an inch off the sheet and fell. She cooed over my flower offering.

"Bleeding hearts are my favorite," I told her as I arranged the flowers in a plastic cup on her bedside table. "Then lilies of the valley, but they aren't blooming yet. I'll bring them next time, if there is a next time. Not that you're going to … I mean …"

We sat in silence until I remembered the brightly colored get well card the kids made for her. I dug it out of my tote bag and held it up for her to see. She stared at it, her face soft. She never had kids. Instead, there'd been a long line of dachshunds.

As pretty and lively as she was, Aunt Peg didn't marry until her thirty-seventh year. In grade school I had a crush on her handsome six-foot-four, fifty-something boyfriend with silver Brylcreemed hair. I was thrilled when Mom announced they'd gotten married at the courthouse. Something would've been wrong with the world if no man wanted to live happily ever after with my Aunt Peg.

When she drifted back to sleep, I kissed her cheek and tiptoed out of the room.

CHAPTER TWENTY-FIVE
One Down... Make That Two

IN THE MONTHS FOLLOWING AUNT PEG'S SURGERY, I WAS THROWN from a friend's horse, which shredded my anterior cruciate ligament. I had a surgical repair, then developed a blood clot.

With all my own health issues, I somehow missed Mom telling me that my grandmother Mimi was extremely ill. Her congestive heart failure was worsening, so Mom and Aunt Peg moved her into Providence Manor. Right across the hall from Dad, in fact. However, she did not go willingly. Or quietly.

Since Mimi resisted the men who transported her to the home, they had to strap her to the gurney. "I was so embarrassed," Mom said on the phone. "She was screaming. Everyone stared at us."

"Mimi screamed? I don't ever remember her raising her voice."

"Did she ever. 'Get me out of here!' and 'I hate nursing homes.' And 'I want to die in my own bed, in my own house.' It was awful."

My poor, beautiful, soft-spoken Mimi. When I asked if she was okay now, Mom said that, according to the nursing home director, Mimi had stopped almost everything except for breathing.

Two weeks later, Mimi was gone. In the funeral home before her memorial service, I watched my Catholic relatives from New England kneel on the prayer bench near Mimi's casket. I closed my eyes and pretended to pray also, but really I was apologizing to Mimi for not having the nerve to go up front and kiss her cheek. "I miss you already. I'm sorry you didn't get to die in your own home."

As Chad and I waited for the hired pastor to arrive, we discussed how Mimi loved that all our kids had brown eyes, just like hers. She adored Lark's dimples because they, too, were just like hers.

Chad turned toward the entrance to the room. "Did you say Jude was or wasn't coming in for this?"

My fingers dug into his pants leg. "Is he here? Do you see him?" Heart pounding, I searched the crowd for Jude's blue eyes and shiny curls. It wouldn't surprise me if he showed up.

A few years back, Jude had flown in for Mimi's ninetieth birthday celebration. Knowing he'd be there, I hadn't wanted to go, but I couldn't think of an acceptable excuse for missing it. Recalling my oath to keep him away from my family, I informed Chad we'd be leaving the kids at home with a babysitter.

At the restaurant, I led Chad to an empty table, where I hoped we could make an appearance but not actually engage with anyone. And there, across the room, tan with white teeth that flashed when he smiled, sat Jude. My cousins surrounded him, drinking beer and conversing jovially.

Before dinner was served, when Chad went to the bathroom, I felt a slow panic build. What if Jude tried to talk to me? What would I do?

One of my cousin's perky daughters skipped over and climbed into the chair beside me. "Why aren't you talking to Jude? He's your brother, you know."

I mumbled as I pretended to search for something inside my purse. A moment later she scampered away. I wondered if Jude sent her. What was taking Chad so long?

As soon as Chad walked through the restroom doorway, Jude moved toward him. I waited for Chad to punch him. Instead, they chatted for fifteen minutes, maybe twenty. I didn't speak to Chad for the rest of the night.

After Mimi's funeral, the whole family drove to her house one last time. Mom, Aunt Peg, and their little sister, my Aunt Mae, suggested each grandchild choose something of Mimi's to remember her by. I walked from room to room, trying to decide what I wanted.

Finally I carried a delicate set of cordial glasses to Aunt Peg. She was resting with her eyes closed in Mimi's beige brocade recliner in the Wedgwood-blue living room. When I tapped her hand to ask for the crystal glasses, she didn't open her eyes. "Take whatever you want. Whatever's left will be auctioned off. Better for you to have it than a stranger."

I set the glasses carefully on the nearby mantle and returned to Peg's side. Her face was gray-green like it had been right after her surgery. I crouched beside her. "Aunt Peg, are you okay?"

"I feel like crap. My vision's weird. I'm getting a migraine."

I brought Mark over to check on her. He asked a few questions then held up three fingers. "How many do you see?"

"Two. No, four." Mark turned her face to the lamp to peer into her eyes. "Is it back?" she asked.

Mark knelt beside her. "Tomorrow, call your doctor and tell him to schedule a CAT scan. As soon as possible."

Aunt Peg's hunch was right. What had started in her ovaries had migrated to her brain. Her vision was blurring because a tumor now pressed against her optic nerve. Her oncologist scheduled her for brain surgery.

A few days before Aunt Peg's operation, the kids and I drove down to visit her. She wanted us to meet the kittens a wild mama cat was raising on her front porch. The drive down was lovely. Cool air and warm sun. Glorious fall color painted the hills.

Aunt Peg and I relaxed in woven, webbed lawn chairs, sipping sweet tea while the kids romped on the porch floor with the kittens. The mama cat warily watched our activity from the edge of the yard.

After a bit, Aunt Peg whistled softly to get my attention. Whispering, she made me promise to find the kittens good homes. When I insisted she was going to make it—I was sure of it—she told me to stop talking nonsense. So I promised. She nodded, her gaze on the tops of the evergreens at the edge of her property.

Aunt Peg was sleeping when I stopped by after her second operation. Though her head was bandaged, I could tell the surgeon had shaved some of her shiny bronze hair. When she woke, her eyes searched the ceiling, unfocused and panicky. I clomped my feet as I approached her bed to make sure she knew someone was there.

"Hey, Aunt Peg! How are you?" As soon as they left my mouth, I regretted the words.

"Not so hot." She groaned and tried to roll away from me. "The surgeon isn't sure he got it all."

Beside her bed, I gulped. "I'm so sorry to hear that. I'll be sure to pray for you."

She turned toward me then, quickly, her brow rumpled and her eyes slightly crossed. "Well, when you pray, pray for me to see again, because right now I can't see a damn thing!" As she reached up and patted her head, her fingers traveled from cloth to curls to skin. "Tell your mom I want a closed casket. I don't want anyone to see me like this. Got it?"

"Oh, Aunt Peg, please—"

Her mouth clamped down. "I mean it."

A few weeks later, Aunt Peg asked me to come fetch the kittens. Now that they were weaned, they could leave their mother.

When I arrived at Aunt Peg's house, I was relieved to learn her vision had returned somewhat. She could now see up to six feet away. Some of her hair had grown back too. Her makeup was almost perfect.

As soon as she finished packing a plastic grocery bag with kitten supplies, she looped the handle on my wrist and led me to the front porch, where she kissed each kitten on the nose. Once they were settled into their traveling box, Peg slipped an arm around my waist and squeezed.

"Thank you for doing this. It means a lot."

I lifted the box onto the picnic table and set the supply bag beside it. Before I turned around, I blinked my eyes so they wouldn't leak. "Is there anything else you need?" She shook her head. I gave her a hug and tried not to let go, but she extracted herself gently. Silently, I gathered everything and headed down the flagstone path.

After I settled the kitten box on the front passenger seat, I walked around to the driver's side of the car and paused for one last look at my aunt waving to me from the front porch of her cute little cottage among the evergreens and ferns. I blew her a kiss she couldn't see and honked the horn as I backed out.

I never saw Aunt Peg again.

CHAPTER TWENTY SIX
Grief

NOT LONG AFTER AUNT PEG'S MEMORIAL SERVICE—WHICH JUDE thankfully did not attend—Mom phoned, saying she didn't feel so good. "I'm shaky. I can't sit still. My insides are churning. I don't know if I can hold it together. It's so much. First Mimi, then Peg."

Forcing a cheerful tone, I suggested she call her psychiatrist. "You probably need your meds adjusted."

When Mom spoke, the edge had bled out of her voice. "Why didn't I think of that? Will you take me?"

At the doctor's office, her psychiatrist wrote a prescription to improve the quality of Mom's sleep and appetite. He murmured approval when I suggested a grief support group. Still, Mom stayed slumped in her chair.

Back at the house I flipped the switch beside the gas fireplace to wake the flames. Mom settled into her recliner and clicked the television to The Weather Channel. In the kitchen I added her new medicine to the lengthy line of amber bottles on the counter.

Outside I collected her mail and newspaper. As I stacked them on the side table next to her, I spoke briskly. "Now, Mom, it's important for you to eat, drink lots of water, and get plenty of sleep. We don't want you to end up in the hospital."

Handing her the cordless phone to keep close, I told her I needed to get on the road. She lifted her chin, and I noticed her eyes shone with tears.

I dropped to the floor next to her chair and rested my hand on her knee. I explained that all the things she was experiencing—sadness, inability to sleep, lack of appetite—were grief issues. "Mom, these things don't mean you're going crazy."

She stopped twisting her tissue. "That's good to know."

"You should journal like you used to," I suggested. For decades, Mom had filled dozens of spiral notebooks with who knew what. Probably her frustrations with life, with Dad, with us kids. Perhaps her hopes and dreams.

I offered to bring her a book on grief so she'd know what to expect in the weeks to come. She nodded but continued to sniffle.

"I'm sorry you lost your mother and sister so close together. With Dad not doing great, all this must be hard. Are you lonely?"

"Yes." Her voice was a whisper. "I wish I was closer to God."

It took me a moment to recover from surprise and formulate a response. "I'm glad you want to be close to him. My faith definitely helps me through hard times."

"Oral Roberts was on television the other night," Mom said, her eyes shut. "He said a prayer, and I said it with him." A tear slipped down her cheek, and a wave of compassion caused my whole body to soften.

Sweet memories came to mind, recollections of fun times with Mom. As much as I dwelled on the bad times, there had been some good ones. The way we used to sit side by side on the living room sofa as she taught me to embroider dresser scarves. I tried so hard to get my French knots as pretty as hers. Sometimes, in the afternoon, she let me watch soap operas with her. In the living room, she'd lie on the olive-green sofa while I sprawled on the floor, under the rainbow afghan she'd knitted.

Every year, out in our backyard when the weather warmed, Mom showed me how to care for the lilies of the valley, zinnias, and Shasta daisies. On summer mornings, our Keds sneakers left green dashes in the silver dew as we made our way to the pussy willow bush on our property's edge. Mom smiled as she stroked the furry catkins. "They look like kitten paws, don't you think?"

I loved when Mom took me shopping and how in between department stores, at McCrory's five-and-dime, we'd order club sandwiches and made-in-front-of-you cherry Cokes. "This is the ticket," Mom always said. "A little bit of caffeine'll perk us right up."

My favorite thing was when we dressed fancy and drove downtown for lunch at the Elephant Room. As the sweet ancient waiter with shiny mahogany skin scooted in my chair, I gave him a shy smile. Under the snowy tablecloth I watched my patent leather Mary Jane shoes dangle above the plush crimson carpet.

When the waiter asked for our drink orders, I crossed my gloved hands in my lap and smiled up at him. "May I have a Shirley Temple, please? With two maraschino cherries on a pink plastic sword?"

I don't remember Mom telling me no much. "Since I'm in fourth grade now, may I please have my birthday party at the roller rink?" I asked her one night as I sliced green olives for the dinner salad.

"That sounds fun."

While we watered the garden one morning, I presented my heart's desire. "May I please take horseback riding lessons? A half-hour lesson is only ten dollars."

"I think we can manage that."

"I've had my driver's license a month now. Is it okay if I take the car tonight?"

"Ask your father."

"May I go to Myrtle Beach with Suzy, Stretch, and Natalie after graduation?"

"We'll have to see about that. Is it okay with their folks?"

The sound of Mom sniffing returned me to her living room. Checking my watch, I stood up. "I have to go, Mom, but remember, you're not alone. God's here with you." Feeling warm from the memories, I wrapped her in an enthusiastic hug instead of my usual air-kiss goodbye.

As I drove home, I felt hopeful. Would our future conversations be easier since we now had something in common besides Sophia, Lark, and Wyatt? Maybe Mom would stop criticizing me. Perhaps I'd stop saying things that hurt her feelings. What was that one saying? "Anything is possible with God."

CHAPTER TWENTY SEVEN

Three Down

The last weekend of the year, Chad and I drove the kids to a cabin in Ohio. For three days, the five of us hiked hills and explored forests and caves. We roasted hot dogs and marshmallows in the cabin's stone fireplace, and we soaked in the roomy hot tub on the back deck.

At midnight on New Year's Eve, after an impromptu dance contest, we sprinted outside in our pajamas, hooting, banging pans with wooden spoons, and howling at the darkness as the old year departed. While the kids frolicked in the frosted grass, I considered how different this New Year's Eve felt than the year before.

"This has been the best weekend ever," Sophia declared as Chad and I tucked all three kids into the king-sized bed in the cabin's loft. Chad and I exchanged satisfied grins.

When we returned home from our weekend away, a message from Mark waited on the answering machine. The director of Providence Manor had contacted him to report that Dad had become unresponsive. I immediately called Mark and told him I'd drive down to check on Dad first thing the next day.

In the morning when I arrived at the nursing home, Mom was already in Dad's room, sitting in a corner chair, flipping through a magazine. The scene made my heart hurt. Why wasn't she beside Dad, holding his hand and murmuring sweet nothings?

Pulling another chair close to Dad's bedside, I kept him company as he slept. A tube snaked from his nose to an oxygen tank on the floor. I placed my hand on his chest and felt the racing of his heart.

"Are you trying to stay alive, Daddy?" I swabbed the inside of his mouth with water and rubbed lotion on his flaky arms. I combed his still-black hair until it shone. Hours later, I told him and Mom I needed to get the kids off the school bus. "But I'll be back tomorrow. I promise."

As I walked out to my car, it occurred to me I'd probably see Jude soon. My hands shook as I unlocked my door.

Thinking Dad would probably pass soon, Mark drove up the next day to meet me and Mom at a funeral home to make arrangements. The young owner gave us a tour and detailed the available services. He suggested that when the time came, we display mementos of Dad's life—photographs, diplomas, uniforms—in and around the memorial service area. I volunteered to provide a bottle of Pabst Blue Ribbon beer and a can of Spanish peanuts. I told Mom she should bring his telegrapher keys and diplomas. Mark added that we could make a photo collage.

Our host asked if we knew Dad's preference: burial or cremation? We answered as one. "Cremation."

An hour later in a nearby Italian restaurant, I nibbled garlic bread while Mark and Mom jotted a to-do list on a napkin. Mom asked Mark to call the cemetery.

"You're going to bury him even though he's getting cremated?" I said, scrunching my nose.

"I want him in a cemetery where I can visit him, not in my house."

Mark's phone rang. I could tell from his side of the conversation it was the nursing home. Mom was pale as Mark switched off his phone. "He passed five minutes ago."

Mom dug in her purse for tissues and handed me one. "I want to go home."

"Do you want to visit Dad one more time?" Mark asked me.

I nodded. I wanted to tell Dad goodbye.

Back at the house, Mom lay on the sofa with a Kleenex in her hand, staring at the ceiling. She assured us she'd be fine and made shooing motions.

In my car, I followed Mark to the nursing home. I whimpered the whole way, fixated on the notion that the next time I bought a car, I wouldn't be able to ask Dad for his opinion. He'd never check *Consumer Reports* or the *Kelley Blue Book* for me again. Glancing at the gas gauge, I grinned. He always snuck a twenty-dollar bill in my back pocket for gas, even when I was grown.

"What will I do without you in the world, Daddy?" I asked the night sky.

CHAPTER TWENTY-EIGHT
Brace Yourself

THE NEXT FEW DAYS I MOSTLY STAYED IN BED, SLEEPING AND crying softly. Remembering.

Mark phoned from Mom's house. We agreed that even though Dad hadn't recognized or spoken to any of us for at least two years, his death still felt like a shock. Mark planned to stick around another day to order Dad's death certificates so Mom wouldn't have to.

After we hung up, I sorted through the dozens of sympathy cards on the foyer table. It was a comfort to know so many people cared. I didn't feel as sad as I expected. I missed Dad, but I knew he wouldn't want to go on with his body working but his brain not.

For a brief moment, I considered denying Jude entry to our father's memorial service, but the idea quickly flew away. Dad was Jude's father too. As uncomfortable as I knew the day would be, I didn't feel I had the right to withhold the opportunity for Jude to say goodbye to Dad, to his ashes.

Anxious as I felt at the time, I believed the day to be something I'd have to simply gut my way through. Few in attendance knew our family's secrets and sins. What was the harm in pretending to be functional for one more day? Even so, I detested the idea of Jude inhabiting the same space as my children, possibly even conversing with them. I anguished over their occasional curiosity about Jude. Inside my mind, I cautioned them, "Do not trust him! He's dangerous!"

The night before Dad's memorial service, Chad and I watched *The Return of the King*, the third movie in *The Lord of the Rings* trilogy. I paused the DVD to tell Chad that I felt like Eowyn, the warrior princess.

"Tomorrow I face the thing that scares me the most!" I declared, my voice a whine.

"You'll be awesome," Chad assured me.

After the movie, I checked email. There were several messages from friends and one from my brother Tom. He wasn't coming in, he wrote. Why should he? He never really felt part of our family.

As Chad brushed his teeth, I told him about Tom's decision. Chad said it was just as well, because who knew what would happen if Jude and Tom were in the same room together.

Several times, Tom had told Chad and me the story about the last time he'd spoken to Jude. Once while visiting California, Jude called Tom's house several days in a row, letting the phone ring over and over. The last time he called, he left an ominous message on the answering machine. "Pick up the phone, Tom. I know where you live."

As soon as Tom heard that, he snatched the receiver out of the cradle. "I own a gun, Jude, and if you ever set foot on my property, I will use it."

So yes, it was probably good that Tom would not be there.

Before turning out my bedside lamp that night, I looked up the Bible story about the reunion of Jacob and Esau years after Jacob betrayed his brother. The prospect of seeing Esau terrified Jacob. I imagined myself as Esau and Jude as Jacob. I wanted Jude to feel terror in my presence. I have the power now, Jude. The power is mine.

The morning of Dad's service, Chad left early for work. Less than an hour later, Lark crept upstairs, climbed in bed with me, and soon fell asleep. As I lay next to her, it occurred to me Sophia and Lark might be afraid of Jude. A few years back, when I felt they were old enough, I'd explained what had happened between me and Jude to both girls. I taught them about safe touch and unsafe touch and "no means no." "Any time someone says or does something that feels bad or wrong to you, run. Yell. Find me or Daddy or a grownup you trust."

When she awoke, Lark pelted me with questions. "What does he look like? Have you forgiven him? Are you going to be nice to him?"

Suddenly Sophia appeared beside the bed. "That's what I want to know too!"

The phone rang. It was Mark, so I sent the girls downstairs to get dressed. Mark said Jude had arrived the night before with his girlfriend. I wrinkled my nose. Jude had a girlfriend?

I tried to sound casual. "So, what's up? What have you all been doing?"

"I asked if he was sorry for what he did to you," Mark said abruptly.

I pulled my knees to my chest. "You did not! What did he say?"

"He said he wants to make things right with the family." I didn't respond. "I don't know if he'll have the guts to say anything to you, and if he does, it probably won't be in the nice pretty package you want."

"So?"

"So, can you just be kind?" When I didn't answer, he continued. "You know there was pornography in the house."

As soon as Mark brought the topic up, I pictured my parents' bedroom in our childhood home. I heard the scrape of a wooden dresser drawer opening, felt the cool slipperiness of my mother's white nylon panties, recognized the powdery fragrance of sachet cubes wrapped in gold foil.

My fingers found the paperback book. I pictured the cover illustration—a pen-and-ink drawing of a man hunched over a teenaged girl. She wore a thigh-high pleated skirt and lacy white ankle socks with shiny black Mary Jane shoes. The girl's face was flushed and her eyes wide. The man's expression combined menace with pleasure. In each chapter, the man violated the girl, his niece. He insisted that though she cried no, her body said yes.

I recalled thinking, every time I opened the book: This gave Jude the idea. This gave him permission.

There were magazines too. I never saw them, but Tom had mentioned them to me several times.

"Yes," I told Mark through tight lips. "I know there was porn."

"And he did drugs."

"I know that too." I wanted to tell him to stop making excuses for Jude, but my mouth wouldn't work.

"Also, I'm sorry, for that one time." His voice was a scratchy whisper.

I wasn't sure what he was talking about. We'd done so many things together in our younger years. What exactly was he referring to?

Still miffed at his excuse-making on Jude's behalf, I acted like I knew what he was apologizing for. "Oh that," I said. "I forgave you for that a long time ago."

His exhale was grateful.

After he hung up, I allowed myself to feel my feelings. Mark and Valerie hosting Jude and his girlfriend vexed me, but then, Mark's ability to forgive Jude, and forget the multiple ways he had devastated our family, had surpassed mine for decades. His "can you just be kind" request reminded me of Dad's words all those years ago: "Try to be your cheerful and good-natured self." For the sake of appearances, Dad and Mark, my whole family, had always wanted me to play nice with the person who wrecked my childhood.

And yet, a part of me relished the chance to play the martyr that day. I'd throw kindness and grace Jude's way like confetti. Only I would know my goodwill wasn't entirely genuine. That part of me still wanted him to pay for what he did.

When Chad returned home from work, he stretched out on the bed next to me while I went over what Mark said about Jude.

"What do you want to happen now?" Chad asked. "If this was a story, what would you write?"

I closed my eyes and imagined the scene. "I don't know. Maybe he'd approach me and say, 'I'm sorry.' Or 'Will you please forgive me?' You know, something like that."

"It might not happen exactly like you want."

I nodded as Chad stood and held out his hands. I grabbed them and he pulled me into a hug that felt like armor.

CHAPTER TWENTY-NINE
Brother and Sister

AFTER CHAD WENT DOWNSTAIRS TO READY THE KIDS FOR THE DAY, I took extra time with my makeup, wanting to be beautiful for my daddy's memorial service. I slipped into a new dress of gauzy maroon, then stepped into matching pumps. A necklace and earrings with red stones completed my ensemble. I sprayed my favorite perfume, then stepped through the fragrant mist.

Hearing a car horn honk, I watched from the third-floor window as Chad loaded our children into the car. Before going downstairs, I surveyed myself in the mirror one more time. I wasn't shaking. A small victory.

When I climbed in the car, Chad whistled softly. "You look great. Are you ready?"

I showed him my hands, fingers crossed and palms pressed together. "I think so."

A few blocks from the funeral home, Chad leaned toward me. "How are you now?"

"Nervous, but peaceful." I murmured. He wanted to know how that was possible. I shrugged. "I have a feeling today will have a happy ending, but getting there will probably be stressful."

"I sure hope you're right," he said as we pulled into the funeral home's parking lot.

"Who's that weird man?" Lark blurted as she climbed out of the car. In the middle of the parking lot, my Uncle Frank stood squinting at the sky, eyes bulging behind thick bifocals. As I waved at him, I hissed at Lark to stop her giggling. Mark had recently informed me our uncle lived with schizophrenia, which explained why he had sometimes seemed odd to me. Why had no one told me sooner?

Spotting my cousin Ellen and her family, I told my kids, "Last time I saw Ellen was at my Granny's funeral. Lark was in my belly then."

Ellen hugged me and expressed her condolences. As we walked, we introduced our families to one another. Inside the funeral home, I excused myself to set up the room for Dad's service.

In a corner, I located our two boxes of photographs: Dad as a little boy, him and his brothers, Dad in his Navy uniform, Mom and Dad's wedding picture, the high school senior portraits of me and my brothers, snapshots of the grandkids. Sophia offered to help so I gave her Dad's framed diplomas to arrange on a nearby table. Each time the door opened, a surge of panic whizzed through me. Was it Jude? Friends of mine arrived, several people I didn't know, then finally Mark and his family with Mom. I spoke with them briefly then returned to the staging of Dad's mementos.

Ten minutes later, Jude appeared. Heart pounding, I studied him and his girlfriend before they spotted me. Jude still looked handsome, with hair clipped so short his curls were gone. He was gray at the temples now, his eyes a winter sky blue like Mom and Dad's, like mine. Behind him, his elegant girlfriend stood, tall and blonde.

As soon as Jude saw me, he headed over. I glanced around for Chad. Where was he? I felt stiff, frozen, unable to run in the event I needed to. The situation felt all too familiar. Help, please, someone!

A moment later, a gentle composure settled over me. I felt warm and gracious.

Jude threw his arms around me and pressed my face into his decades-old rust-colored corduroy sport coat.

I coughed. "Let me go. I can't breathe." I smoothed my dress and nodded toward his girlfriend. "Who's this?"

Jude introduced the woman as Angie. I wondered if Angie knew. About Jude and me. About Jude and Tom. Probably not.

Chad joined us, the kids peeking out from behind his back as he greeted Jude. Watching my husband accept my estranged brother's extended hand, I frowned. There it was again, Chad's ability to put family before everything else. Even me. How were so many people able to let Jude off the hook? How did everyone so easily forget my pain? And Tom's?

Jude gawked at the three of them: Sophia fourteen, Lark ten, and Wyatt six.

Lark gripped her hips. "Take a picture. It'll last longer."

Jude laughed. "I'm sorry. It's just that—you all are so big."

As more people arrived, I hurried to finish adding photos to the magnetic display board. Jude asked if he could help. I nodded. Each time he handed me a picture, his hands shook.

I grinned at a portrait of Dad with his four brothers. "Do you remember how whenever Uncle Frank visited, Dad made him sleep in the basement on the pullout sofa with that thin mattress and poky springs?"

Jude chuckled. "And Dad would hide the kitty litter box underneath so it would smell to high heaven and Uncle Frank wouldn't stay long." He waved me away. "Your friends are waiting for you. Go. I'll finish this."

During the memorial service, I sat on the front row to Mom's left while Mark and Jude sat on her right. Chad and the kids occupied the row behind us. Early in the service, Wyatt fell asleep, tipping slowly sideways until his head and shoulders rested in Chad's lap. After everyone was seated, Sophia walked to the front of the room with her flute and performed a beautiful rendition of "Amazing Grace."

Lark leaned forward and whispered loudly. "Just so you know, Uncle Jude is crying."

After Mom and Dad's pastor spoke, cousin Ellen, an ordained minister, offered a prayer of comfort. Then she asked if anyone wanted to share stories about Dad. Mark told of his respect for Dad as a father. Two of Dad's brothers—Uncle Jim and Uncle Robert—told tales about their family living through the Great Depression.

I considered sharing some memories of Dad, but when I glanced over at Mom, she looked wilted and blank-faced in her chair. She'd heard enough Dad stories for one day. I patted her knee. "It's almost over."

To close the service, Ellen led us in the Lord's Prayer. Lark's breath warmed my neck. "Just so you know, Uncle Jude knows the Lord's Prayer."

For the family meal after Dad's service, Mom had reserved the private party room of the nearby Italian restaurant. Two long tables stood side by side. I sat at the end of Mom's table with Chad and the kids. Jude and Angie ate at the other table with Mark and his family. Our aunts, uncles, and cousins filled in the remaining seats. For a while, everyone was quiet, but after a little wine and coffee, the room buzzed with conversation.

A little after eight o'clock, Lark tugged my sleeve, announcing it was time to go. She stood and addressed the group. "We have to leave now. It's my best friend's sleepover birthday party tonight."

Wanting a moment alone, I told Chad I'd collect our coats. In the hall outside the private dining room, sconces with cream linen shades cast luminous circles on the striped wallpaper. The carpet printed with cabbage roses muted my footsteps, as well as the sounds of laughter and silverware clinking. I paused at a mirror to inspect my reflection. I recognized relief on my face and in the way I held my shoulders.

The coatroom smelled of perfume on wool scarves and winter coats stored with mothballs. I found and slipped into my coat then piled the rest of our family's outerwear over my arm.

When I turned around, Jude stood there in his dated blazer, emanating drugstore cologne. Out of habit, I took a step back to increase the distance between us. He edged into the small space—casting a glance over his shoulder—all wine breath and nervous sweat. I shrank into the wall of coats behind me where all sounds were silenced. In the dim light, Jude's teeth flashed white.

With a dramatic sweep of his arms, he bowed and asked to have a word with me, his voice breaking like a teenager's. Did he call me Madame? The scene felt weird, almost funny. I inched toward the doorway, but he stepped in front of me, wringing his hands.

"I just want to be your big sister again. I mean, your big brother. I'm sorry. For everything."

Dazed, I nodded slightly.

"Yes, you accept my apology?" he gushed, his entire face so very hopeful.

I nodded again, afraid to say too much too soon. It would take more than a few sentences to right all the wrongs between us. Plus time to prove him worthy of trust. But this was a start.

"I have to go. Lark has a slumber party."

In one movement, he grabbed me, plus all the coats, and lifted the entirety off the floor. In his arms I stayed stiff, still wary of his touch. He dropped me abruptly and pushed the coat pile at me. "All right. Goodbye. See you around."

At home, the girls and I hurried into the house while Chad freed Wyatt from his booster seat. In the foyer, we tossed our coats on the settee and climbed the stairs.

"So?" Sophia said from her spot on Lark's daybed.

"So?" Lark said as she balanced a pillow on top of her sleeping bag.

I'd been quiet the whole ride home. I lowered myself onto Lark's tiny desk chair and told the girls what happened in the coat closet. "But don't tell Daddy. I want to."

Lark hugged herself. "I like Uncle Jude. He's funny. And handsome."

Sophia nodded. "He's not what I expected at all."

"Come on," Lark said, grabbing my wrist. "I'm going to be late."

On the way downstairs, she turned to face me. "I just thought of something. I know why Doc died. He died so you and Uncle Jude could be brother and sister again." I gaped at her, but before I could respond, she skipped through the door with her little pastel suitcase and Disney sleeping bag.

My wish came true, I realized later as I settled into bed. But was "I'm sorry" enough to make up for all those years? Had Jude really changed, or did he just tell me what I wanted to hear?

After Chad listened to my account from the coat room, I asked him what he thought. Was Lark right? Could Jude and I be brother and sister again?

"Let's just wait and see, shall we?" Chad said, as he turned out the light.

A month later Jude called, causing my stomach to seethe like in the old days. I guess I'm not totally over what he did, I thought.

"Can I get your kids' social security numbers?" Jude asked a few minutes into our call.

My eyes narrowed. "For what?"

"If it's okay with you and Chad, I want to name them as beneficiaries on my insurance policies, since I don't have kids of my own.

You don't have to tell me right now. Talk it over with Chad and get back to me."

I recalled what he'd said in Cincinnati all those years ago. "It's all about family. You guys have it and I don't." Maybe this was him, trying to make restitution. Trying to make us all a family again.

"You know what? I don't need to ask Chad. I think it's awesome you want to do this."

"Really?"

"Really."

PART FOUR

The Unraveling
2002 & 2015

CHAPTER THIRTY
Mad Mom

LESS THAN A WEEK AFTER WE MOVED DAD INTO THE NURSING HOME in the summer of 2002, Ron from Home Health Angels contacted me. Thinking Mom might be apprehensive alone in the house without Dad, Mark and I had arranged weekday companion care for her.

"Might want to check in with your mom," Ron said. "Seems to me, she's exhibiting paranoid behavior."

When I dialed Mom, she asked if the Angels were bonded and insured. Her tone sounded like leaves stirring before a storm.

Chad, the kids, and I were headed to a wedding that weekend, so I suggested to Mark we book an Angel to stay with Mom Saturday and Sunday. Mark said there was no need. He'd drive up and stay with Mom. It would save us a couple hundred bucks.

Late Saturday night, the phone in our hotel room rang. In a panicked voice, Mark said Mom was freaking out. I told him to calm down. He was a doctor. How bad could it be?

"For the last hour, she's been running door-to-door telling the neighbors I'm after her. She's trying to get them to let her in, probably so she can call the police on me."

I promised to phone Mom. When she answered, I ignored the

bite in her voice. I shared a few wedding details, then asked if she wanted us to stop by on our way home the next day. She said that would be great, that hopefully Mark would be gone by then.

Mom seemed fine when we visited her in the afternoon, but Sunday evening Ron contacted me again. Mom had called the police on one of the Angels. She swore the woman stole her considerable stash of U.S. savings bonds.

An hour later, on the sidewalk in front of her house, Ron told me that as soon as the police had arrived, Mom recanted her accusation. He requested a list of Mom's medications, saying he needed to know what he was dealing with for the safety of the ladies he sent over. That's when I realized what was happening. Recently, after thirty years of her taking lithium, Mom's psychiatrist refused to refill her prescription. Ron asked why.

I waved him away from the car door so I could open it. "Something about liver damage, but you know what? With her being seventy-something, we can live with the possibility of liver damage. It's the psycho stuff we don't want to deal with."

Two days later, one of Mom's neighbors called. That morning when she stopped by Mom's house, one of the Angels had let her in.

"Your mother locked herself in the bedroom and refused to come out. After a few minutes, I convinced her to open the door. On the floor beside her bed were a half dozen five-pound cans of peaches from Sam's Club. Jean handed me one and said, 'If that Angel woman comes in here, bash her in the head.'"

That afternoon I phoned Mom's physician, a Dr. Jenkins. Hearing the details, he recommended that Mom be hospitalized. After learning there were no available beds in the hospital psychiatric ward near Mom, he suggested I take her to the psychiatric hospital in my town. There was a catch, though. In order to have her admitted, I'd need a referral from the emergency room by eight o'clock that night.

"How would you like to go in the hospital for a few days?" I asked Mom over the phone. I tried to make it sound like a party invitation.

"To stay for a while?" Excitement tittered in her voice.

"Your doctor thinks it would be good for you."

"It was Dr. Jenkins's idea? Then, yes. I'd like that." There it was —her Nubain voice.

Two hours later, in front of Mom's house, I tapped the horn. She scurried out with her suitcase and purse. As I opened the trunk, I asked about her little dog and she pointed next door. Good job, I told her.

Soon after, it began to rain, a gray sheeting downpour. I hated driving in the rain, especially in the dark, and night was falling fast.

Halfway into the trip, Mom spoke to her window. "You know that woman in North Carolina who drowned her kids? I know what that feels like."

My breath drained away. When did you become like this, Mom? I thought. Then I remembered how years ago, someone had said Mom was fine until Jude was born. It made sense.

Mom's heavy exhales painted the window a milky white. "When you were first born, your father took the boys camping. I didn't know what to do with you. I wasn't sure that I wouldn't … hurt you."

My grip tightened on the wheel. You meant to say kill me, didn't you, Mom? Please tell me this stuff isn't hereditary. Cracking the window slightly, I sucked in gulps of cool, moist air to keep from hyperventilating while I mouthed the words, "She almost killed me. My own mom almost murdered me."

The closer we got to the hospital, the twitchier Mom became. Whenever she glanced over at me, her eyes seemed to glitter. She flipped her sun visor up and down.

I checked my watch. It was after seven. "We won't make it," I murmured.

Mom whipped to face me, her mouth savage and tight. "What does that mean?"

I pictured myself speeding all over West Virginia—up and down steep grades, through dense mountain laurel thickets, sliding over onto the berm with a spray of gravel as I navigated sharp turns in the fog and pouring rain, driving from hospital to hospital. "Will you please admit my mother?"

"My mom's having a nervous breakdown," I called out as we finally crossed the threshold of the emergency room. At the nurses' station, I pressed my forehead against the plexiglass and spoke to the woman on the other side. "Is there a more politically correct term I should use?"

The stout nurse held out her hand, palm up. "Insurance card and photo ID?"

As I dug in Mom's purse, a young nurse holding a thermometer approached. Mom opened her mouth like a baby bird. "They'll know what to do here," Mom assured me, her teeth clacking on the thermometer.

After the nurse checked her temperature, she cheerfully pronounced Mom normal. I rolled my eyes. The check-in nurse tapped the window with her pen. She pointed to the waiting room and told us to stay there until Mom's name was called.

In the holding area, I patted the blue chair beside mine. Mom sat. Surveying the room, I was relieved to see no blood or vomit, no bones poking through skin. One guy, huge and hairy, reminded me of Grizzly Adams, the burly, bearded man from the TV series I loved as a child. Clearly he had the same condition as Mom. With thumbs hooked in the straps of his bib overalls, he danced a do-si-do in front of his people.

Mom stared intently at the right corner of the room where the wall met the ceiling. Then the left. She leaned forward and pivoted her head to see behind her—first one corner, then the other.

I patted the magazine in my lap. "Look here. It's Oprah and Dr. Phil. You watch them, right?" I could distract her for a few seconds, then she'd resume the owl ritual. As people began to stare, I stopped looking up. "Check this out. Is this Kathie Lee Gifford?"

Suddenly, Mom twisted her head. "They're coming for us." Mad energy radiated off her. "We won't make it out alive!"

Staring at my knees, I considered making an announcement: "For the record, we're not related. She's not my—"

"For God's sake, you're my only daughter. Run, Dina. Save yourself!" With surprising speed and agility, Mom bolted toward the exit. The electronic doors sprang open.

I sprinted after her. "Someone help!" I ran to the check-in window and crouched to speak through the opening. "Call security!"

With a manicured finger, the nurse marked her place in her book. "Your mother came in of her own free will. We can't force her to stay."

I smacked the glass. "Are you kidding? Look at her. She's nuts!"

The nurse crossed her arms. "I just follow the rules, you know."

Mom screamed from outside. "Run for it, Dina!" She paced left and right, causing the doors to stutter open and shut. "This is our only chance to make it out alive."

A tall man in dark slacks and a cream sweater approached Mom. Draping one arm around her shoulders, he whispered in her ear. Mom beamed as she asked if he was a doctor. He was. Her body melted into his and she smiled up at him, blinking coyly. My stomach heaved.

He raised an eyebrow at me before nudging her inside and down a hallway. I followed a few steps behind. In front of the pastoral counseling room, he told her to wait inside. He'd make sure a doctor saw her soon.

Mom faced him, her eyes bright. "A doctor will know what to do."

At one thirty in the morning, Mom swore she heard something. "Check the hall. You still have time. Save yourself. Go!"

"I'm not going anywhere, Mom. I won't leave or forsake you." No doubt the spiritual reference would be lost on her, but still, it made me feel like a good daughter.

When an elderly man in head-to-toe khaki appeared in the doorway, Mom shrieked and covered her head. Smiling warmly, the man said if we were hungry, he'd bring us each a meal from the cafeteria.

I devoured my burger, fries, and slaw and took long pulls of slushy pop straight from the can. Mom huddled over her tray, dividing her attention between her burger and the door.

Soon after, I heard footsteps in the hall. Mom stiffened. In the doorway, a tall, solidly built young man appeared. His skin was smooth and tan and his hair shiny black. "Is someone not feeling well?" he asked, revealing perfect white teeth. I pointed to Mom. Her eyes climbed his form.

"Are you a doctor?" she asked.

"Resident." With a word, I knew he was not from West Virginia, not from the United States. His cologne was familiar. Ralph Lauren Polo, the same as his shirt.

"Here's the deal," I began. "My mom's manic-depressive, bipolar, whatever you want to call it, and her psychiatrist, out of the blue, yanked her lithium after almost thirty years and—"

"I know what you want." His words were clipped. "However, there is one small obstacle. There are no beds up the hill at St. John's."

No beds? I sagged. Now what?

"So," Mom said, her voice silky, "how much longer do you have in med school?" She tilted her face up at him. "I was a registered nurse, you know."

The resident excused himself and when he returned several minutes later, he informed us he'd spoken to Dr. Jenkins. Lo and behold, there was now an available bed for Mom. He'd send men to transport her.

Up at St. John's, a young man admitted Mom and offered to keep her purse and any valuables inside the hospital safe. When she didn't respond, I answered for her, "Yes, please. That would be great."

"Unfortunately, you won't be able to visit her until Tuesday," he said as I signed a form.

"Darn," I said.

It was four o'clock in the morning when I left Mom. Away from the glow of the hospital lights, I skipped to my car, singing the opening lines of Napoleon XIV's "They're Coming to Take Me Away, Ha-Haaa!" The song from my youth, describing an individual's descent into madness, seemed fitting.

CHAPTER THIRTY-ONE
Home Again

Four days later, I didn't want to leave my bed. But I had to get the kids ready for school. And I had to be a good daughter.

How many times had Dad endured this same scene? Mom had been admitted to the hospital at least twice that I could recall. Since Dad always acted calm and matter-of-fact during Mom's transitions from home to the hospital and back, it never seemed like a big deal. He was always cheerful when he took us to visit her. In the car on the way, he'd remind my brothers and me to be sure to admire the things she made in arts-and-crafts therapy—colorful plastic suncatchers, whipstitched faux-leather coin purses. Dad accomplished the process so effortlessly, whereas I felt like an incompetent understudy with a bad attitude.

In the common area of Mom's floor at St. John's, I spotted her alone at a long table, her lunch tray untouched. She was still performing the owl ritual. She wasn't fixed.

Seated across from her, I said hello twice, but she didn't respond. Perhaps she was sedated. I snapped my fingers in front of her face. Nothing.

"How's the food?" I asked. She didn't answer. What a waste of a week, I thought. If she didn't speak in five minutes, I'd leave. She never said a word.

On the way out, I stopped at the nurses' station to see if there was anything I should know. "Your mother tried to escape earlier today, around noon," the nurse told me. She leaned over the counter and pointed. "See those doors down there? She went right through them, swore they were the doors to heaven."

Two days later, Mom was better. Too much so.

The group therapy facilitator approached the table where Mom chattered and I pretended to listen. "We just love your mom. She's such a pro in group, we might give her a job." Turning her head so Mom couldn't see, she gave me a sly wink.

As she walked away, another woman joined us—Mom's caseworker. She wanted a word with me in private. In her office she announced she had good news. Mom would be released in the next few days, possibly as soon as the weekend. Wasn't that great?

"But it's not even been a week. She can't be fixed—I mean, better, already. I was with her that night. You can't undo that kind of damage in seven days." The woman mumbled something about insurance. "Forget insurance. Mom can pay out of pocket, no problem." I attempted a smile. She didn't reciprocate. I dropped my eyes, hoping she'd reconsider. Please keep her another week. Or a month. Or forever.

The next day, as I signed her discharge papers, Mom pecked my shoulder and asked for her checkbook. I spoke without turning to her. "Why are you asking me? I don't have it."

"I handed you my checkbook when I came in here and you know it. Now where is it?"

I told myself to stay calm, to not engage. "Don't lie to me, Dina. You wouldn't steal from your own mother, would you?"

Moments later, the nurse placed Mom's handbag on the counter. I shoved it at her, suggesting she search inside. Her fingers wrapped around the checkbook. I wanted her to raise her eyes to see my I-told-you-so face, but she didn't. She hugged the bag to her chest and headed for the elevator.

The next week I drove Mom to meet her new psychiatrist. I liked him, the way his voice rang with a gentle lilt from somewhere outside the United States. After a few minutes of small talk, he covered Mom's hands with his and asked if the last few months had been hard.

She sniffed and nodded. "Call me Jean."

He scribbled two prescriptions—one for lithium and one for a sleep aid. "These will make a world of difference," he assured us. Mom glared at my noisy sigh of relief. From his desk drawer, the doctor produced a business card. "After all you've been through, with your beloved husband no longer at home with you, I think it would be wise for you to see a therapist." Mom didn't respond. "It would, of course, only be for a few months." He nudged the card toward her. "Will you do that, Jean, for me?"

Next to me, Mom was stiff. At last she picked up the card and tucked it in her purse, in a compartment she never used.

Inside the car, Mom crossed her arms. "What do I have to talk to a therapist about?"

I listed a number of potential topics: Dad's relocation to a nursing home, her kids not speaking to one another, her recent exodus from a psychiatric ward. "I'm thinking you have enough material for months, if not years, of therapy."

"But why do I have to talk to a stranger?"

At the next stoplight, I faced her. "I've got to be honest with you, Mom. I don't like when you to tell me intimate details about your marriage. I'm your daughter and Dad's. Telling me private things about your all's relationship is a conflict of interest. Don't you see that?"

"I didn't mean to put you in an awkward position," she said through her teeth. "I just thought we were sharing."

Sharing, she called it. I focused on the red light and tried not to laugh.

After her first counseling session, Mom called, insisting therapy was a huge waste of time. She had no desire to "air her dirty laundry" to a stranger.

"Mom, counselors work with screwed-up families all the time. Dysfunctional families are normal. Trust me. We're not the only ones."

"I don't believe that for a minute," she said. Then she hung up on me.

A week later, Mom phoned again. With a whole new attitude about counseling. Her words ran together as she informed me her psychologist wanted me to attend some sessions with her. I sneered. I did not want a stranger probing around in my head trying to determine my feelings for Mom. I recalled Chad's advice. "I'll think about it and get back to you," I promised.

I let Mom simmer for a few days before I called to say I would not be accompanying her to counseling. To my surprise, she didn't seem to care. In fact, she sounded giddy as she announced there was something else she wanted to discuss.

Her therapist had another patient she wanted Mom to meet—a man, a widower. The psychologist thought it would be good for him and Mom to spend time together. "He misses his wife. I miss Paul."

Mom cut into my silence saying she knew the man, sort of. He attended her church. He was quite handsome and—

"Uh, Mom? Dad's not dead."

She huffed. "I know that, but my counselor thinks it would be good for me. She says who knows how long Paul will live. It could be years. She told me I can't put my life on hold forever." Mom informed me she planned to speak with my brothers too. She wanted us to consider this possibility and let her know how we felt. I figured Mark would be against it. Tom too, but knowing Jude, he'd be fine with it.

That night I dialed Mark. Without saying hello or how are you, I asked if he knew what Mom was up to. He said she'd called him the night before. I frowned. She told Mark before me?

Mark called the psychologist's plan an affront to Dad. He intended to remind Mom of her vow forty-eight years ago to love Dad in sickness and in health, until death do they part.

After we hung up, I decided to write Mom a note. As I hunted for stationery and my fountain pen, I told myself that putting my thoughts on paper did not make me a communication coward. I simply wanted to get the wording perfect.

Dear Mom:

You wanted to know how I feel, so here goes. I am not comfortable with you spending time with another man when Dad is not dead. Besides that, I think it sends a really bad message to your grandchildren. I don't know if you've considered the fact that if you go out with this man, you'll be committing adultery. I think that fact would really upset my children. You wanted my opinion; there it is.

Two days later Mom phoned. Since Mark and I didn't like the idea, she would not be going out with the widower from her church. As I hung up, it occurred to me there was an upside to the whole situation. If Mom felt like dating, it probably meant she was doing better emotionally. That was something.

CHAPTER THIRTY-TWO
The Fall

IN THE SUMMER OF 2015, I DARED TO BELIEVE THE DIFFICULT STUFF was behind us. The kids, Chad, and I were all doing beautifully. Then one day, Chad, Wyatt, and I returned from the county fair parade to find three messages on the answering machine. Mom had fallen in her home, used her crisis call alert system, and was now in the emergency room of the hospital in her town. I quickly packed an overnight bag and drove down.

Back at her house, Mom had to grip my arm to walk or stand. It didn't take long to figure out that she was unable to accomplish any life function—cooking meals, dressing, or going to the bathroom—without assistance. Her hands trembled so much, she couldn't even feed herself. My mother could not be alone.

I stayed the night, and first thing the next morning, I called her physician. The office was not yet open so I left a voicemail summarizing Mom's condition and requesting a home health recommendation. Though I meant around-the-clock companion care, Mom's doctor phoned in a referral for her to receive skilled services: registered nurse, physical therapist, occupational therapist, and a home health aide to bathe her.

In addition, his office suggested that Mom see her psychiatrist, since her sudden decline seemed possibly connected to a recent change in medications. The next day at the psychiatrist's office, Mom was referred to a neurologist.

When an EEG showed no evidence of a stroke, Mom sighed with relief, but I sagged with disappointment. A stroke would have gotten her admitted to the hospital.

The next day I drove the forty miles home to pack more clothes, my phone charger, and books. Trying not to cry, I hugged Wyatt. "She can't be alone. I shouldn't have left her this long, but she promised she wouldn't move from the sofa."

Wyatt patted my back. "We'll be okay, Mom. Go."

Each morning at 6:30, I heard Mom talking to her cat, Rosie. It was her way of telling me she was ready to start her day. If I didn't respond immediately, she'd call out. "Dina? Are you up? Can you hear me? I have to go."

In her room, I folded back the covers and swung her legs to the edge of the bed. Gripping her wrists, I pulled her to sitting. Together we took tiny shuffling steps to the bathroom, Mom clutching my arm. I had to center her over the toilet or she'd lower herself too far right and miss it. Once she had a firm grasp on the nearby safety bar, I'd hurry out of the room. In case it was number two.

"I'm done," she called minutes later. I always delayed slightly—unkindly, I knew—but I did it anyway.

"Did you wipe? Okay, let's wash your hands. Now sit at the vanity. Here are your top teeth. Are they in? Good. Now your bottom ones. Do you want your hearing aids today, or not?"

In the bedroom, I settled her into the small blue barrel chair beside her bed and held up a pair of khaki pants. "Do you want a blue top or green?" After that I opened her dresser drawer and selected a pair of full-cut silky white underpants. I brought her a Playtex bra too—the same style she'd worn for as long as I could remember. From another drawer I chose a pair of Peds, tiny beige footies.

"Don't forget my shoes," she reminded me each day.

"Mint green or pastel blue?" I asked from inside the closet.

We always got her underwear and slacks on first. I arranged both items at her ankles and brought everything up in one motion. Using the arms of her chair for support, Mom pushed up as I made sure the elastic waistbands on both items lay flat.

She held her arms straight out for me to put on her bra. As she leaned forward, I struggled to close all four of the hooks and eyes. Next I snuggled her breasts one at a time into the bra cups. I lifted their weight, left then right, up off her ribs, then inside the respective white spaces.

"Why didn't I inherit your big boobs?" I asked her more than once, trying to distract myself from the fact that I was touching my mother's breasts.

There were moments I felt incredibly tender, all warm tapioca pudding inside. This is what a good daughter would do. I'm such a good person.

Other times I hated what I had to do. Please God, let today be the day I arrange around-the-clock care because the sameness of these days is killing me. Then in my mind I'd ask for forgiveness. For being such a lousy daughter.

On the seventh day at Mom's, I phoned the Home Health Angels. I didn't care if their services cost thirty dollars an hour. I needed to go home now. Ron answered my call.

"Remember me?" I asked. I explained Mom's decline, told him how skilled home health services were in place and helping, but that Mom needed 24/7 companion care. He promised to assemble a team as soon as possible.

"Like, how fast? Wyatt turns sixteen on Friday. I haven't shopped for his presents. I don't know what kind of cake he wants."

"Let me see what I can do. Maybe I can get someone out there tonight. No guarantees, though."

Please, please, please be tonight, I prayed.

Two hours later he called back. "How about tomorrow morning?"

"My hero."

CHAPTER THIRTY-THREE
The Jugular

By September's end, Mom's physical improvement was miraculous. At her request, I toured a senior living facility in my town and added Mom's name to the waiting list.

"The complex is beautiful," I assured her when I called. "The chef used to work at a country club, and for five dollars, you can learn ikebana, the Japanese art of flower arrangement. Every Thursday, they host a guest lecturer. And it's very tastefully decorated. You'll love it."

"I just want to make one friend, you know?"

"I know, Mom. I know." I recalled how not long ago, she'd confided how hard it was for her to form close friendships with women.

I promised when her physical and occupational therapy sessions ended, I'd bring her up for a tour of the place.

"Will you still take me out every now and then?"

"Of course."

A month later I terminated the night shift of Home Health Angels after Mom confessed she wasn't waking them up to take her to the bathroom at night. I also stopped driving down twice a week to do her grocery shopping and errands. "You and the Angels can do that, right?"

"Yes! I'm going stir-crazy in this house."

I was encouraged that she wanted to get out again. She seemed so much healthier, in every way. But a few days later, as I drove her to the eye doctor, she attacked me.

"What are you on today? You're all keyed up. You and that Anna Angel." She made a yakking motion with her hand.

In search of the doctor's office, I scanned the signs on either side of the road. Here we go again, I thought. Lately I'd hoped Mom had somehow changed during her crisis, that maybe she and I formed some kind of special bond, but no.

"Actually, Mom, this is who I am."

"You talk too much. And too loud. You're not like this all the time."

After I parked the car, I faced her. "Do you know why I'm not like this all the time? It's because I know you don't like who I am. So I tamp myself down most of the time. I make myself less to make you happy."

I was proud of my honesty, loved the way Mom's mouth hung open and her eyes got huge. I imagined my words like tiny daggers, lined up at eye level in front of her face, aimed at her unkind, unmotherly opinion of me.

"I'm like your father," I added. "The Irish salesman. I'm like your sister Mae. You're always saying she talks too much too, that her diet pills must be speed. And I'm like Jude. He and I are both loud and high energy, and you're not. You hate that."

"I can't get a word in edgewise," Mom grumbled. That got me. There was truth there.

"You don't like me, Mom. You don't love the woman I've become."

As I spoke, it occurred to me that Mom seemed incapable of unconditional love for me. As far back as I could remember, whenever I didn't fit her perfect daughter mold, she let me know.

"You wear too much black. You always look like you're going to a funeral. At your age, your hair should be short, not long. You do too much for your kids. Why don't you visit me more?"

I looked her straight in the eye. "You don't like *or* love me, do you?"

Mom didn't answer. She didn't protest that of course she liked me, of course she loved me. Her silence confirmed that she would only consider me worth praising if I looked and behaved exactly how she wanted.

Though it was a hard truth, I recognized it as her opinion, which she was entitled to. Honestly, it didn't even hurt all that much. Over five decades, I'd grown calloused to the absence of my mother's acceptance.

Less than two weeks later, we battled again.

"You're angry," she said not long after I arrived at her house. "I'm not a mind reader, but I can tell, your feelings toward me have changed."

She had no idea what she was doing, the effect that spouting all her favorite psychology phrases, the ones I despised, would have on me. Five minutes in her presence, and my stomach was at high tide.

Mom also didn't know what I'd promised Chad that morning.

"Do not let her be mean to you," he said. "Promise? I'll bawl her out again if I have to."

"You will not speak to my wife the way you have been lately," Chad had told Mom on the phone a week prior. "With your sons in Texas, California, and on the other side of the world, Dina is the only one who has your back. I can assure you, she only has your best interests in mind. Since the Angels are at your place every day, there is no need for Dina to phone you or come down for several days. If you have an issue, you call me."

Chad had phoned Mom because I was both devastated and enraged by her attacks on my character. She said I hadn't taken her out of the house in months. She didn't recall important financial arrangements she had agreed to. She even called Mark and tattled on me.

To his credit, he texted me as soon as he hung up with her. "Been there, done that. I support everything you're doing."

Until Chad gave me the gift of a week off from caregiving, I had no idea how exhausted and angry I was. At first I was anxious. Would Mom have another nervous breakdown? Would I have to take her back to the psych ward? But when the phone didn't ring at all the next day, or the next, I told Chad, "Thank you so much! I am loving my week off."

After Chad's imposed silence ended, Mom behaved herself, but not for long. I had planned a girl getaway trip, but when Mom pouted, I canceled it.

"Why didn't you go on your trip?" she asked as I sat at her desk, paying her bills.

"Because I didn't want to make you mad."

She stammered, saying that had never been her intention. After I brought her mail in, she suggested we go out to lunch.

Picking up my purse and keys, I said, "Fine, where do you want to go?"

"Applebee's."

"We went there last time," I said. "I'll decide the place." I drove toward the mall. We'd go to the restaurant there with a shrimp entrée Mom liked.

"We haven't been out to lunch since this summer," she commented along the way.

"Yes, we have, Mom. Applebee's, ten days ago."

"That is not true."

I did a U-turn in the middle of the road and hissed at her. "This is not happening. I will not take it, you treating me this way, calling me a liar."

In her lap, both hands gripped her purse straps. Her mouth made its nervous clicking sound. "You've changed, I knew it, your feelings toward me. You hardly ever come to see me now."

No doubt I'd earned this. During her health emergency, by visiting her every other day, I created in her an addiction for my presence. Once she was better, I sharply tapered off my visits. I had to. The deep well of compassion I'd felt for a time was now dry.

"Wyatt is back in school," I explained. "He has activities every day after school and he plays in the band at the football games on Friday nights. Plus I'm writing and editing for a friend." I didn't mention the friend was me.

She dabbed at her eyes with a crumpled tissue and when she thanked me for my explanation, I regretted giving her a reason to feel the relief that settled into the folds of her face.

"But you have changed," she said softly. "You have. This summer—"

My voice became brittle. "This summer when you were in crisis, sick and fragile, you were nice to me. Now that you're better, you're mean again." Inside my chest, I felt a blender of emotions skip straight to puree. "Nothing I do is ever good enough. You don't like my hair. I don't visit enough. You are such a bitch."

When her jaw fell, the lines on her face smoothed out for a moment, subtracting a decade, but then they bunched up again and I regretted my cruelty to an old woman.

Her words were weak. "You've never spoken to me like this."

Oh please, I thought. I'd felt this fury before, the way my temper filled the car, making the air hot and close. The day I told her and Dad the things Jude did to me, I'd used the f-word at least twenty times.

For the first time ever, she wept in front of me. I was stunned by the realization that though I'd heard her whine and lament, I'd never seen my mother cry real tears. It was as though she was disappearing in the seat beside me, a genie going back in its bottle. And yet, I felt no compassion. Surprise, but no mercy. Actually, it was an invitation to wound again.

"Of all your kids, you love the pedophile best."

Her faded blue eyes bulged. "That is not true. Oh God ..."

"I'm sorry. I shouldn't have said that. That's what Tom believes, not me."

I wanted to point out that, like the old saying goes, I was her bird in the hand, that her three boys were all in the bush, and that I was pretty sure they wanted to be there because it was far from her and her insatiable desire to be thought well of no matter what, far from her efforts to make our misery equal hers.

Back at the house, Mom headed straight for the bathroom. I told the Angel on duty we'd fought and that I was leaving. "Be nice to her. She's bound to be upset."

"You're the only one who's ever stood up to her," Chad said later that day in the living room when I described the brawl.

"Mark did, that one time in the restaurant in Fairview. Remember? When she threatened to cut us out of her will if we didn't take her to Myrtle Beach?" Chad said this was different. "Can I read something to you?" I asked. "On the way home, I bought the book *Boundaries*. This explains everything." I found the pages I'd dog-eared, the ones identifying me as a "compliant" and Mom as a "manipulative-controller."

After I read the section aloud, I stretched my legs over Chad's on the sofa. "I was going to lie and tell her I was going back to work full-time and would only be able to see her on the weekends, but I came up with something better. This book gave me the idea. From now on, I won't visit her alone. I'll take you or Wyatt with me. That way she won't be mean to me and I won't react to her in anger. Plus, there will always be a witness to what she says and how many times we visit."

"That's an excellent plan," Chad said as he massaged my legs. "Way better than lying."

CHAPTER THIRTY-FOUR
Aunt Mae Talks

THAT FALL, MOM AND I TOURED THE ASSISTED LIVING FACILITY near me and she loved it. I studied the faces of the directors of marketing and residential living as I listed Mom's psychiatric medications. They didn't flinch. They only asked how often lithium blood levels were checked.

Two days later we met with Mom's financial adviser. He assured her she had enough money to live comfortably for another twenty years, if not more. When he left, I asked Mom if she was pleased with the numbers.

From her recliner she whispered, "When the money's all gone, what then? Will you all put me out on the street?"

"Of course we won't. It's a nonissue, anyway. Did you not hear the man? You have enough money for twenty years, Mom. Maybe more."

"I don't have any spending money, and I need to pay the girl at the beauty salon. I want you to bring me some blank checks. Bring my jewelry back too."

At the counsel of several friends, and with Mom's permission, I'd taken all of her valuables to our house before home health services began.

I stood. "I'm going to go now."

She smirked. "Where's your person you said you'd always bring with you?"

I nodded toward the front door. "That was the financial guy, and he just left."

Later that day I recounted the incident to Mark over the phone. "Maybe there's more going on besides her bipolar disorder," he said. "Perhaps she also has borderline personality disorder."

After we hung up, I Googled the condition. The indications sounded right: paranoia, fear of abandonment, alternating between demonizing and idealizing loved ones. The root of borderline personality disorder was thought to be childhood abuse or neglect. I read that sentence again. Had Mom experienced either?

There was only one person who might have the answers: Mom's only living relative, her sister, my Aunt Mae.

A few days later, I phoned Aunt Mae. I explained how Mom had been acting lately and about Mark's borderline personality disorder theory. A psychiatric nurse for years, my aunt said she hadn't spent enough time with Mom recently to feel confident diagnosing her. But when I told her about the boundaries I'd set, she said, "If you feel the need to set boundaries with her, she probably does have borderline personality disorder."

"Was Mom abused or neglected when she was little? I read that can be the cause."

"Funny you should mention that. Lately she's asked me several times if Daddy touched me. No, he never touched me. He was never home. He was always at the Elks Club. Since Jean and Peg were tight and always off doing their own thing, I was usually stuck home with Mother. Mother never hugged or kissed us, but I never doubted she loved us. Now she—our mother, your Mimi—was abused."

I'd suspected as much since Mimi had told Mom abuse happens in every family. "What happened to her?" I asked.

Aunt Mae described the time Mimi had been outside with her sister Hester and their mother, Kate. That day, Mimi and Kate watched helplessly as Hester was hit and killed by a runaway truck careening down the hill in front of their house.

After Hester's death, Kate became so depressed, she was unable to take care of Mimi. As a result, Mimi was sent away to live on a farm. Mimi's parents thought maybe if their daughter worked all day helping the farmer's wife, she'd fall into bed at night and the horrible dreams she'd been having would cease.

One day Kate visited Mimi at the farm. As she glanced out the window of the farmhouse, she saw a boy with his hands up Mimi's dress. Kate took Mimi home that day and never returned. Years later, Mimi told Mae how the farm boys would say to her, "Pretend you're a cow and we'll get on top of you."

I moaned. "Poor Mimi. It happened to me and Tom too. Did Mom ever tell you about Jude abusing us?"

Mae said Mimi told her, not Mom. "Why didn't you tell someone?" my aunt asked.

There it was, the dreaded question. I told her I didn't think anyone would believe me. I worried they'd blame me. Plus, what boy would ever want me if he found out what I'd been through?

"Of course," she said, sounding sorry she'd asked.

"When did Mom change? Was she okay growing up?"

"Oh, Dina, before you kids came along, your mother was the best person, always doing things for people, helping other kids at school with their projects. Whenever Peg was mean to me, Jean took my side. She always cried when Peg and I got spanked."

Aunt Mae told me Mom helped her get ready for her prom and assisted her on her wedding day. "Your mother told me, 'You'll have the rest of your life to get dressed with your husband.'"

I couldn't imagine Mom doing those things, saying those things. I wished I'd known that woman.

"Your mom changed when she had kids. It started after Tom was born."

"I thought it was after Jude's birth," I said. "Was it postpartum depression?"

"Maybe. Probably. She weighed eighty-two pounds after he was born."

I gasped. "Eighty-two pounds? How is that possible? I was with her when she told her doctor she weighed 145 after nursing school." Aunt Mae said it was the mania.

"But Mom told me she didn't think she was ever manic, only depressive."

Aunt Mae laughed. "Did we ever see her manic! When I visited her, or when Peg did, we could always tell which phase she was in. If everything was clean and the kids' faces were scrubbed shiny and Jean was super skinny, she was in a manic phase. If everything was a mess and the kids had spaghetti sauce all over their faces and Jean was heavy, she was depressed."

Mae went on to tell me about the time Mom was so mad at Dad, she took a Greyhound bus up to stay with Mimi.

"I remember that! She took me with her. I still remember the dress she wore." I recalled how the fabric felt on my cheek—silky and thick— when I laid my head on her lap. "It was blue and white check. I loved that dress."

"Your dad sent her roses because he wanted her to come home."

"How did Dad put up with her all those forty years? She was awful to him."

Aunt Mae's voice softened. "Oh, Dina. Your father really, really loved your mother."

I didn't remember seeing that kind of love. Jolly affection maybe, but not a deep love like Aunt Mae described.

"Initially they put your mom on Elavil to stabilize her, but then lithium came out. When they put her on that, she was like a new person."

I switched subjects. Knowing that Jude had lived with Aunt Mae and her family for a time, I asked if she ever saw anything unusual, sexually inappropriate maybe, while he stayed in her home. Or maybe my cousins had witnessed something.

She didn't remember Jude doing anything bad. "Jude's bipolar too. You know that, right?" she said. I had guessed that, and more than once, Mom had told me she was sure of it. "And hypersexuality is part of mania, you know," Mae added.

I sat up. "Hypersexuality?" I'd not heard that word or come across it during my research. In the notes I was taking during our conversation, I wrote the word and circled it. I glanced at my watch. We'd talked for two hours. "Thank you so much for telling me all of this, Aunt Mae. Please don't tell Mom we talked. She'd be furious."

CHAPTER THIRTY-FIVE
Hypersexuality

THAT NIGHT I RESEARCHED MANIA AND HYPERSEXUALITY. IN *The Diagnostic and Statistical Manual of Mental Disorders*, hypersexuality is listed as one of the primary symptoms of bipolar disorder.[1] It may occur in 25 to 80 percent of all patients with mania.[2] It is often the most destructive and challenging part of being bipolar. Symptoms include preoccupation with sexual thoughts, out-of-control sex drive, increased use of pornography, excessive masturbation, and inappropriate and risky sexual behavior.[3]

I also looked up hypersexuality in children and found that 30 percent of bipolar children present with hypersexuality before puberty, as do 60 percent of children who have reached puberty.[4] That could explain how, even as young as ten or eleven, Jude abused Tom and me.

All the articles I read cited parental reluctance to report this behavior. For a time, hypersexual activity was linked to abuse, and parents feared if they told their physicians, their child might be taken from them. But in a groundbreaking study of hypersexuality in children, Dr. Barbara Geller found that only 1 percent of hypersexual children studied had been sexually abused.[5]

One article spoke of siblings being pulled into games of Doctor.

Some parents reported, during periods of hypersexuality in one child, that they watched all their children "like hawks." Most understood their children should not bathe, shower, or sleep together. They also knew separation should be imposed as soon as signs of hypomania and hypersexuality were observed.

I wished my parents had known instinctively to watch Jude like a hawk instead of ignoring him. No wonder Mark demanded to leave the boy bedroom. What had he seen or experienced there?

I felt almost elated. If my theory was correct, Jude's hypersexuality explained his ongoing sexual abuse of others. It didn't pardon him, but it illuminated the cause. It was possible no one abused him. That those urges were always in him. I felt something akin to relief knowing there might be a medical reason for what he did. He was subject to an insatiable sexual appetite, driven by mental and emotional chaos. I had to wonder, did he even have a choice?

As if being hypersexual wasn't enough, it seemed he was also attracted to children. Was he a true pedophile or were we victims solely because of our proximity to Jude when hypersexuality struck him?

I considered the similarities between Mom and Jude. Both were bipolar but loathe to admit it. Both were terrified of being abandoned in old age. Yet, both were often horrible to their loved ones. What was life like with that much torment inside?

CHAPTER THIRTY SIX
Wisdom

TWO DAYS LATER MOM ACCUSED ONE OF THE HOME HEALTH Angels of stealing. After the young woman phoned in a report to the office, she left Mom's house in tears.

Over the next few days Mom's accusations increased. "She stole twenty dollars, maybe more. No doubt she's been stealing from me for months. I bet she's planning to burn my house down!"

Mom called so often, I turned the ringer off on my phone. So she began phoning Mark. When she once called him ten times in one day, he picked up and told her to stop harassing him.

She continued to call me, then Mark, then me again. She informed Mark that Chad was the reason for all the trouble we were having. No doubt he was jealous of the time I spent caring for her during that summer, so now he was poisoning me against her. Mark advised her to discuss the issue directly with Chad.

The next morning when I checked my voicemail, there was a new one. "Dina? May I please speak with Chad?"

"I had to remind her I was mad at her because she was hateful to you," Chad said the next day after speaking with Mom. "She keeps forgetting that part. But by the end of the conversation, she was begging me to smooth things over between you two. She said I'm the only one strong enough to fix this mess. Oh, and she told me she doesn't want to go into the senior community up here because they don't allow cats. I promised to find her another place."

Though Chad thought the conversation went well, Mark texted me later in the day to say Mom called him to reiterate her Chad-is-evil theory.

"She's headed for another breakdown," I texted Mark. "This is exactly what happened ten years ago."

After supper, I assured Chad I could handle committing Mom again, if necessary. Having been through it once, how bad could a second time be?

Because she left multiple voicemails that day, I called her back before Chad left to take Wyatt to karate. I put her on speaker phone so he could hear the conversation.

"I have two liars and criminals in my life," Mom announced.

"Oh my gosh, Mom. Who?"

"You and Chad."

"You need to see your psychiatrist, Mom. And you need your meds adjusted."

"You're the one who needs a psychiatrist!"

"Remember your Life Alert System, Mom, the pendant around your neck. If you feel unsafe or out of sorts tonight, press that."

She hung up on me.

The next morning, despite my bravado the night before, I wept for over an hour. I wasn't so much distressed over my relationship with Mom as I was terrified to relive the process of committing her to the hospital. So much for my recent confidence on that topic.

Between bouts of tears, I blizzarded Facebook with prayer requests—on my personal wall, on a page dedicated to prayer requests, and on our church's wall. I also emailed three friends from high school to ask them to pray.

One gal replied within the hour, saying her mother—a friend of

Mom's from years ago—believed she knew the root of Mom's struggle. Curious, I called Mrs. Fisher later that afternoon.

Her accent was Georgia thick. "Your mother's been on my mind for the past few days. The Lord showed me she has an idol in her heart. I can't see exactly what the idol is, but until she repents of it, the enemy has legal permission to torment her." She also told me to release all my past, present, and future hurts regarding Mom.

"I have, Mrs. Fisher, but they keep coming back!"

The next morning, I phoned the office of Mom's psychiatrist to tell the staff I was fairly certain she was headed for a psychotic break.

"Is she threatening to harm or kill you?" the office manager asked. I said no. "Is she a danger to herself?"

"I don't think so."

"Then there's nothing you can do."

To be honest, I wasn't sure if Mom was going insane or simply being combative. Seeing her in person would answer that question. Knowing an Angel would be with her that day until two o'clock, I drove down for a visual.

When I rang the doorbell, Mom let me in and introduced me to the Angel on duty. Mom was dressed and wearing makeup. Her living room was tidy, with the television tuned to the news. Mom appeared quite sane.

On my way out of town, I stopped to tour the senior living community a few miles from Mom's house. The staff and residents were very friendly. And pets were allowed. There was even a bar with happy hours on Tuesdays and Fridays.

"There's a two-drink limit though," the vivacious sales manager told me, "so we don't have scooters and wheelchairs colliding."

When I left, they had my deposit check.

Driving home, I recalled my conversation with Mrs. Fisher. "Your mother has an idol in her heart."

In an instant, I knew what it was. Mom's idol was money.

"Give it back, the pile in your living room. Give it all back to her." Unbidden, the words entered my mind. And they made sense.

In many of Mom's voicemails, she insisted I return her things. Because the pile in my house represented so much wealth, I ignored her demands. I thought returning her items while she seemed emotionally unstable would be irresponsible. But she hadn't appeared crazy when I visited. Her eyes weren't glittering. Plus, she still had the help of the Angels. They could drive Mom to the bank, if necessary.

That night, I didn't tell Chad I planned to return Mom's things. There was no way he'd agree with my decision. If Mom mishandled the items, how would we pay for her long-term care?

But I felt certain Mrs. Fisher was right about Mom's idol, and I was fairly confident the command to give everything back came from God.

After supper, I called Mom from our basement so Chad wouldn't hear. "I know you want your financial stuff back. I'll bring everything on Saturday afternoon between three and five o'clock."

"Answer me one question," Mom said. "Why did you and Chad plot against me?"

I hung up.

She called again and left a voicemail. "Are you bringing the savings bonds too? Are you?"

The next morning, I prepared two documents, a letter for Mom and a form for the two of us and a witness to sign. I then asked a friend to accompany me.

In the afternoon, I carried everything out to my car: a shoebox with Mom's good jewelry, two wooden chests with sterling silver flatware, Mom's checkbook, and her firebox. The contents of the firebox included the deed to her house, the title to her car, a considerable amount of cash, her will, and several hundreds of thousands of dollars in U.S. savings bonds.

More than half a million dollars rested in the passenger floorboard of my car. I covered the stash with a blanket, locked the car, and went back in the house.

The phone rang. It was Mark. After I updated him on Mom's status, he asked if there was anything else he should know.

Uncertain as to whether I was doing the right thing, I told him about my conversation with Mrs. Fisher and how I thought God had told me to return Mom's valuables.

After a brief silence, he spoke. "I admit, this terrifies me a little, her in control of all that money. But really, it's not our money or even hers. It's God's. I trust Mrs. Fisher, and I believe you heard from the Lord. All of this tension is really a battle for control. Let me know how it goes."

My eyes widened with disbelief. Mark was cool with all this? Alrighty then!

On Saturday when Mom answered the door, she looked frail. I introduced her to my friend as we both carried a chest of silver to Mom's dining room table. Once all the items were brought inside, I explained what each thing was and told Mom to be very careful with the one and only key to her firebox.

I held up a pen. "We're all going to sign this paper saying I brought back your valuables so there's never a question as to whether I did or not." Mom sneered as she snatched the pen from my hand.

When Mom wasn't looking, my friend snapped photographs of the dining room table and its contents. After Mom signed the form, she threw the pen to the floor. My friend and I also signed the document, I tucked it into my purse, and we walked toward the door. Mom did not say goodbye.

"That was tense," my friend said when we stood outside.

"A little bit," I said. I opened my arms like wings. "Man, do I feel free. How about dinner and a glass of wine? I'll buy."

At home that night, a message waited for me on the answering machine. In a haughty voice, Mom chastised, "Dina, I forgive you. You and Chad just got off on the wrong track."

The next day Mom left more messages. A sad one: "How did this happen to us? All this mistrust?" And a furious one: "I can take care of my affairs myself!"

For nearly a week, I didn't hear from Mom at all, then the pitiful calls came. "Forgive me. Oh, please forgive me! I was awful to you and Chad. I know I said terrible things, but I don't remember what all they were."

I decided to write Mom a letter. That way she couldn't defend herself, accuse me, or hang up on me. I listened to all her messages and jotted down her questions on a notepad. In my letter, in addition to addressing each of her concerns, I wrote:

> *Dear Mom:*
>
> *In the last two weeks, I have read four books to learn how to cope with the difficult circumstances between you and me. They've taught me how to set boundaries. That's why I gave you back every aspect of your life. If I make your decisions for you, or with you, and you don't like what happens, you will blame me.*
>
> *I believe you are competent to take care of your affairs. I hope having your financial resources back in your own hands will return a sense of autonomy and control to you.*
>
> *You mentioned your desire to remain self-reliant. That's what is fantastic about the senior living facility near you. When I told the sales manager there that you were living alone in your own home, doing everything without assistance except*

driving, she said you would be a great candidate for an apartment in the independent community.

You asked if we could be friends again. Honestly, Mom, that's up to you. These books tell me, in a circumstance like ours, the relationship usually resolves in one of three ways. It eventually returns to normal, is terminated, or becomes superficial.

In closing, I want to encourage you to take responsibility for your physical health, your emotional health, your finances, and your happiness. It is not my job and I refuse to be manipulated into thinking it is. I know these words will be hard to hear, but they're exactly how I feel.

Love,
Dina

Two days later, the sales manager from the senior living community called. "Your mom scheduled a tour on Monday morning at ten."

"That's awesome," I said, and I meant it. I'd grown so much in a short period of time. Now it was Mom's turn.

PART FIVE

The Undoing
2014–2015

CHAPTER THIRTY-SEVEN
Mom's Secret

IN JANUARY OF 2015, SOPHIA WAS IN HER LAST YEAR OF COLLEGE and engaged to be married, Lark was a sophomore in college, and Wyatt a freshman in high school. To participate in the final residency of my masters of fine arts in creative writing program, I'd driven to South Carolina.

At that point, none of us kids were available to Mom. I was eight hours from home, Mark's wife, Valerie, was battling stage-four kidney cancer, and Tom had never forgiven Jude for what transpired between them. So, when Mom panicked, she called Chad. Once I returned, in order to let me catch up on sleep, Chad didn't tell me about their conversation until my second day home.

In the kitchen, Chad moved to sit beside me. "Your mom called one night while I was watching a movie. I let the answering machine pick up, but she sounded really upset, so I called her right back. She was so anxious, she couldn't speak in complete sentences. I tried to calm her down so she could explain what the issue was."

Mom told Chad that during the previous summer, she had walked in on Jude and his four-year-old son, Stephen, in the guest bedroom.

"I had to prod her to continue," Chad said. "She wouldn't be specific about the details, and I tried not to put words in her mouth, but I knew where she was going." My mouth tightened and I shook my head. I knew where Mom was headed too.

"She told me what she saw wasn't right. She said, 'This has been bothering me for a while now and I need to tell someone.' I assured her telling me was the right thing to do and that I would take care of things. Again I asked, 'So you walked in on Jude and Stephen and saw what?'

"She said, 'I saw him doing what he shouldn't be doing, and the look he gave me …' I asked her where Stephen was at the time. She said he was on the bed. I asked her where Jude was. 'He was on the floor. It just wasn't right at all!' Then all of a sudden, she said goodbye and hung up."

The scene Mom described happened during the summer of 2014. Jude, his wife, and their two little boys, Stephen and Will, had flown to the United States from Southeast Asia for an extended visit.

"Mom's eighty-one," I reminded Jude in a Facebook message as he planned the trip. "Two weeks is more than enough to impose on her, especially with a preschooler and a toddler."

Jude promised to leave if Mom seemed overwhelmed.

They stayed nearly three months.

Often during their visit, Mom called me and whispered, "It's been so long. They've been here so long." But she refused to set a time limit for their visit. As long as Jude was looking for a job in the States, they could stay with her. Though she was clearly worn out, I knew Mom would never ask for a break. Still, I told her she should.

"What if Jude gets mad and leaves? Will I ever see the boys again?"

At the end of that summer, after Sophia and Lark returned to college, Chad, Wyatt, and I had driven down every other weekend to spend time with Mom, Jude, and his family. Whenever we visited, Jude cooked for us. Sometimes he even asked in advance what we were in the mood for. It was something he and I shared—the love of food, the preparation, and eating of it. It was also part of his agreement with Mom. While they stayed with her, Jude did all the cooking and cleaning. He drove Mom to all of her appointments too. His wife Leah looked after the boys.

Slender and very shy, Leah was pretty, in a stern and angular way. To my mind, she would have been even prettier and more approachable if she smiled more often. Since she was a native of Southeast Asia, I imagined Leah's reticence was due to her lack of proficiency in English. Or perhaps she felt intimidated when Chad, Wyatt, and I converged on Mom's small house. I made it a point to tone myself down around Leah in order to make her feel more comfortable. Even so, she usually stayed in the guest bedroom with the door closed or occupied herself with giving the boys bites of food or bottles of milk or juice. Or changing their diapers.

Both boys had ebony bowl-cut hair and solemn black eyes. They spoke very little English. During one get-together, Jude announced he'd enrolled Stephen in the nearby FBI preschool. On account of the hydraulic fracturing boom, the area experienced a significant population increase, and all of the local public schools were full. At the FBI preschool and day care, any spots not taken by employees were made available to the public. Jude hoped Stephen's English would improve, and he'd become more socialized. Perhaps he'd even decide to potty train.

That summer Jude and his family showed up at Mom's door in late July, a week earlier than planned. According to Mom, it was early August when she walked in on Jude with his son. Which meant she had kept her secret for five months.

"What are we going to do?" Mom wailed when I called. She

insisted we get in touch with Leah and tell her to never again leave Jude alone with the boys. I asked Mom to describe exactly what she had witnessed, to see if it was the same story she told Chad.

She described how Jude and Stephen had made plans to spend the night in a tent in the front yard. That afternoon, Mom walked into the front bedroom and—

"Was the door open or closed?" I asked.

"It was slightly cracked."

How brazen, I thought. He didn't even shut the door.

"And Jude was … It wasn't right. I could blame the hormones for what he did to you and Tom, but this was sick. It's his own son!" I winced when she brushed off Jude's abuse of me and Tom, and I tried not to picture Stephen's round face and glossy black hair, his strange somewhere-else eyes.

At first Mom's voice shook, but as she continued, her tone grew more determined, as if her jaws were clenched. "I said, 'Stephen, go to your mother. You won't be sleeping in the tent tonight.'"

"I'm so proud of you, Mom. You did the right thing. You stopped him." This time, I thought. Surely it would happen again.

More than once, Jude had informed both me and Mom that he and Leah weren't having sex. He said their abstinence was because Leah was a proponent of the "family bed." I explained to Mom that the term referred to when parents and their children sleep together. "Supposedly it fosters trust and independence."

"The look in his eyes," Mom said, her voice fierce. "He knew he was doing wrong, and he knew I knew it. God! We have to tell Leah." I promised to figure out a way.

We went on to discuss several other incidents that transpired during my childhood, information I'd never been privy to. My eyes burned when Mom divulged details of what Jude did to Tom. Things between the two of them were far worse than I'd imagined.

Before I hung up, Mom asked again how we were going to

protect the boys. I told her I had emailed my friend Trey—a counselor who worked at a nearby school for at-risk boys—to schedule a counseling session. Trey and his wife had been in a church home group with Chad and me a few years back.

"He knows about my past," I told Mom. "And he works with this kind of thing a lot. He'll know what to do."

Two days later I drove to the 200-acre campus where Trey worked. Fresh snow shrouded the property and its narrow, twisting roads. In low gear, I crept down a slick hill on my way to the administration building. At the bottom, I eased my car off the road and parked. With a deep culvert on the right and a creek rushing too fast to freeze on the left, I had no desire to attempt the steep incline to the school.

As I trudged uphill, I flipped up the hood on my parka and arranged my scarf to cover the bottom half of my face. I realized I was climbing this mountain alone to do the thing only I could do. I felt both frightened and brave as I traveled the steep and slippery path. Behind the school building, I cut up a snow-covered bank, grabbing at tufts of weeds that poked out of the snow to keep from falling.

On the front porch I stomped the packed snow from my boots and shoved open the heavy door. Snow dust sparkled the air as I stepped across the spacious entryway. Hanging my coat on a rack, I gave my name to the woman behind the desk. In front of the hearth that reached to the timbered ceiling, I warmed my hands in front of the crackling fire and imagined the heat melting my difficult circumstance.

My friend Trey appeared and led me back to his office. "How are you?" he asked, smiling. "It's been a long time."

"Honestly, I'm not doing great." I provided a quick review of my abuse and enlightened him about Tom's. When I described the recent development involving Jude and Stephen, a shadow fell over

Trey's face.

"How are you doing in the middle of all this?"

I remembered the words I'd written in my journal the day before: "Hate crawls inside you and it wants company."

"It feels as if my forgiveness of Jude is a lie." My voice was unsteady.

Trey shook his head. "You forgave your brother. I know you did. This is entirely different."

"But what about the 'love keeps no record of wrongs' stuff in the Bible? Does that apply here?" What I was about to do would no doubt land Jude in very serious trouble.

"That scripture does not apply in this case. Our number one responsibility is to protect the children. Dina, your brother, I hate to say it, is pure evil. He's a sexual predator. We have to stop him. He has to be blindsided, but by law enforcement, not your family."

As Trey made suggestions, I scrawled notes. "The first thing you need to do is call Child Protective Services in the county where the abuse happened. Ask them what you should do next. The logistics you describe are very complicated. Tell me again why Jude is currently at the South Pole?"

I explained how every year, from approximately November to February, Jude worked as an independent contractor for the government.

Trey squinted at the ceiling. Since the abuse happened in West Virginia, but Jude and his family lived in Southeast Asia, and because Jude currently resided at the South Pole, Trey said my call to CPS might be routed to a supervisor. He recommended several more action items, and together he and I arranged them in priority order.

Finally, he stood and hugged me goodbye. "Keep me updated. I'll be praying."

At home I sent Chad and Tom an email with Trey's to-do list.

Tom had called me the night before saying, "I hardly slept last night. I was filled with dread, but I have no idea why."

"I think I know why," I said.

When I outlined what I knew, Tom cursed softly. "I think I'm going to be sick."

CHAPTER THIRTY-EIGHT
Mom Elaborates

THE NEXT DAY WAS MOM'S EIGHTY-SECOND BIRTHDAY. MY PLAN was to drive down and treat her to lunch. Before I left, though, I needed to call and give a statement to the West Virginia office for child protective services. Trey told me to report both Jude's abuse of Stephen and his abuse of me decades prior. He recommended that Tom file a report as well.

To make sure I included all the complicated details, I wrote myself a script and laid it on the kitchen table in front of me. Before I dialed, I paused. Revealing my abuse to authorities for the first time was daunting. It felt like betrayal—of Jude and my family. For strength, I made myself remember my motivation—to protect Stephen and Will.

The woman who took my statement put me on hold, then came back to inform me that since Stephen and Will were not currently in West Virginia, or the United States, for that matter, CPS could not do anything. Even so, she said my report would be vital when Jude returned to the country.

I also asked if there was any way to add Jude's name to the internet list of sex offenders to protect other children from him. She said he had to be charged first. I thanked her and hung up.

I pictured Jude in a courtroom, wearing an orange jumpsuit, his hands and feet shackled. If they locked him away forever, would he hate me? Would his boys thank me some day? For the umpteenth time, I tried to determine whether I was being righteous or vengeful. Remember Stephen, I told myself. Remember Will.

Mom didn't know it, but I'd planned a special activity for after her birthday lunch. Sitting in her pretty patio home, I told her I had questions about the Jude predicament. And my childhood. I asked if she was okay with me interviewing her. Sure, she said.

My mother is a secret keeper. Always has been. The fact that she was willing to speak up and say things that might lead to serious trouble for one of her children assured me she'd witnessed something dreadful, something she could not explain away.

Before she could change her mind, I asked permission to record our conversation. That afternoon in her living room, Mom agreed without hesitation. She didn't even ask why.

I recorded my name and hers and the date, and asked for her permission to tape our conversation. I wanted to do everything right, in the event we ever ended up in court.

First, I asked Mom about the incident she'd seen between Jude and Stephen. She had not yet been specific about what she had witnessed that day. I rephrased my questions to help her recall the scene with more precision. I tried to be gentle and encouraging and show no judgment. Mom was clearly disturbed by what she'd observed, but her lack of details frustrated me. I was afraid her wishy-washy testimony would come apart in front of a judge or jury.

On the recording Mom also described the only call she'd received from Jude since he arrived at the South Pole for his current contract. During their conversation, when Mom mentioned she'd written a letter to Leah, Jude cut in sharply: "What did you tell her?"

I nodded. "What did you say to Leah in the letter?"

"I just told her how much I missed her and the boys."

I asked another question from my list. "Did Stephen or Will ever act inappropriately during their visit last year?"

Mom gazed out the dining room window, beyond a patch of snowy woods, to the road. Suddenly she straightened. "They went for long drives after school, Jude and Stephen did. They'd be gone for an hour, sometimes an hour and a half. This was after I walked in on them that day."

I pictured Mom's gold Honda Civic wrapped in bright yellow crime-scene tape, with detectives scraping the interior of the car for DNA evidence—the upholstery, the ceiling.

I skimmed my question list. I needed to concentrate in order to block out the image of Jude groping his little boy while Stephen played *Angry Birds* on his tablet.

"Mom, the other day on the phone you mentioned Jude abusing Tom."

Mom didn't flinch. "Tom had moved away when he called to tell me that. It was after he graduated college. He had a job by then."

"Did Tom ever say how many times it happened?"

"No, but it must've been several from the way he talked."

I tried to steady my hands. Growing up, Tom had hated us all: my parents, Jude, Mark, and me. He'd been so alone back then, practically a ghost in his own home.

"Your father sent Tom a book to help him deal with what happened and, you know, tried to talk to him, but Tom only wanted to talk to me. It was just awful."

"Tell me again why Dad brought home Dr. Campbell from the psychology department? What was the point of that?"

"That was for Mark, for when he moved out of the bedroom, but it didn't work. Mark was so loyal to you kids."

I asked Mom a question then, one I'd posed before. "Did you and Dad ever get a sense something was wrong with Jude?"

She thought for a minute, then said no. I reminded her how wild Jude was, how he got in trouble for shoplifting, doing drugs, and sniffing glue. Hadn't he crashed his VW van one night while drunk and ended up in the hospital for a while?

Mom's eyes narrowed. "I told him, 'You're not a juvenile anymore. Any time you get caught doing something bad, you're going to get tried as an adult.' That scared him. He never got caught with drugs again." I couldn't imagine Mom being firm with any of us, much less with Jude.

"So Mark moved out of the bedroom and never said why, which left Tom and Jude in there alone. That's probably when the stuff Tom told you about happened. Was there never a conscious decision to confront Jude about what he did to me and Tom, and what he may have done to Mark?"

This was her chance. I wanted my mother to walk through the responsibility door I opened. Confess, I begged her silently. Apologize.

Mom shrugged. "No. I don't know why."

"Were there other times Jude got in trouble on account of his sexuality?"

Mom stared at the fireplace. "I think … It was … Someone complained about him."

"Who? Someone at school?"

"A mother in the neighborhood called to complain about Jude. She said he raped her son."

"Oh my gosh, Mom, that's awful! Did the parents press charges?"

"Back then? Oh no. No one would ever want it known something like that happened to their son."

I told Mom how my therapist Jamie and my counselor friend

Trey both believed Jude had probably been sexually abused. Mom insisted she didn't remember anything of that nature. She felt certain Jude would have told her if something like that had happened.

We discussed Jude's other son, whom we'd never met. On separate occasions, Jude had mentioned the boy to Mom and me. Supposedly, the child was a genius. Mom said if she remembered correctly, the boy's mother didn't want to have anything to do with Jude, no child support or anything. Which didn't surprise me. Sooner or later, Jude drove off every woman he dated.

I asked Mom if Dad had somehow taught or modeled inappropriate behavior to the boys. "Maybe he shared pornography with them?" Mom didn't think so.

"He was never inappropriate with me," I assured her, "but I thought maybe it was a thing some fathers did—encourage their sons' sexuality." Again, Mom said no.

It was time to redirect the conversation. "When Jude got really unmanageable, that was when you started seeing a psychiatrist, right? I remember your terrible headaches. Is that why you took that one really strong medicine? Wasn't it a barbiturate?"

"I had horrendous headaches back then. It was just … I don't know. Jude drove me nuts. I mean, he'd be on top of a building working, painting, or something, and he'd be taking drugs—marijuana or something like that, you know. He just … He was getting into—I don't know." Mom told me she used to drive to Jude's jobsites to check on him, to see if he was okay. I had no idea she'd done that. It indicated a higher level of function and maternal instinct than I'd given her credit for.

"Were you on a lot of meds back then? To me, you seemed sedated a lot of the time. Like maybe your doctor gave you too many medicines and—"

Mom insisted her psychiatrist did a capable job managing her care. "I told him what Jude did to you," she added. "He said Jude was just trying to learn about girls, and that the issue was between him and you. That you all would have to work it out."

My molars ground together. "That is such crap! Whatever. Tell me about when you got arthritis in your hips a few years back and you refused pain meds. You said you didn't want to be on narcotics because you were addicted to them before."

"I wasn't addicted to narcotics. It was Ativan." For a couple of years, Mom took Ativan for anxiety. "It helped at first, but then I knew something was wrong. I went in the hospital and they straightened me out." I willed my face not to appear shocked. How did I not know this? It must've been one of the times she disappeared from home for a "medication reevaluation."

I asked her what year she'd been diagnosed with manic depression. Mom said she didn't think she'd ever been manic-depressive. She believed herself clinically depressed.

I'd asked my Aunt Peg about it once. Peg thought shopping was how Mom presented with mania. "Have you seen her closet? All those pairs of beige polyester khaki pants with elastic waistbands? Good Lord! How many pairs of khaki pants does one woman need?"

Mom drew the conversation back to us kids. "Your father was a wreck when he found out about Jude and you." She kept her eyes down. "You know, I can truly say I still love him: Jude. I don't like what he's done, though. But we must keep Stephen in mind. We have to get a message to Leah." She sat up and began rummaging through the side table drawer. "I have an address and phone number for her brother. I've had long conversations with him about, you know, Jude and Leah's fighting. And everything else."

So many surprises. "Leah's brother speaks English?"

"Oh yes, definitely. Leah's mother lives there too. I guess Jude insulted Leah's mother something awful and she cried."

I knew about the fights between Jude and Leah, and about Jude insulting Leah's mother. Leah told me. Years ago, she had shared lots of things about Jude, all of them bad.

CHAPTER THIRTY-NINE
Leah Talks

JUDE AND LEAH MET ON A DATING WEBSITE DURING ONE OF HIS contracts at the South Pole. All winter, they communicated via computer. At the end of that particular work contract, instead of returning to the States, Jude traveled to Southeast Asia to meet Leah and her family in person. He stayed with them for a month, then they married.

In November of 2009 when Leah reached out to me on my private Facebook wall, she and Jude had only been married five months. They were expecting their first child. Jude had wanted to wait a few years, but Leah, fifteen years his junior, seemed in more of a rush.

Trying to forge a relationship with my new sister-in-law, I shared some of my pregnancy stories and asked about hers. Leah did not want to discuss motherhood. She wanted to gripe about Jude. In broken English, she typed that she was sick of Jude, that maybe she'd made a mistake in marrying him. She vehemently insisted she was not a "prostitute girl." She said she knew his past and it "really made her sick."

What part of Jude's past was Leah referring to? Surely not what he did to me and Tom. And her using the term "prostitute girl," what was up with that? I'd heard Southeast Asia was known to be a hub for the sex trafficking industry. With Jude's rapacious sexual appetite, had the region proved a paradise for him?

I remembered Tom saying that Jude had bragged to him at one point about renting a house in the Philippines for a month, along with the services of two Filipino call girls. Would Jude have disclosed that to Leah?

Tom also informed me that Jude had forwarded a photo of Leah to him. In the picture, Leah was pregnant. And naked. Her legs were crossed and her arms folded over her breasts, but still. "Isn't she hot?" Jude had asked Tom. Maybe Leah had discovered that email.

"I'm sorry things aren't going well," I wrote. I offered ideas for improvements, but I didn't hear from her again until a year later, after Stephen was born. She begged me to have Mom call Jude. Leah thought Jude might be crazy, the way he was always angry and never respected her family. Apparently she thought Mom had some kind of influence over Jude.

I gave Leah the advice my counselor Jamie had given me. "Negative behavior without negative consequences will never change." I suggested she take Stephen and return to her family. Perhaps Jude would miss her and try harder to be a better husband.

But Leah felt there was no way for her to return home. Her mother would be angry. She'd already insisted Leah try to understand Jude. I felt bad for my sister-in-law. Even though Leah's mother knew that Jude didn't like her, she still took his side.

Leah went on to say that she might leave Jude because of his anger and how he always hit her. She said Mom had her cell phone number. "She can call here."

I contacted Mom immediately and told her to phone Leah right away. I also emailed Leah with more suggestions. Was there a sister or friend she could stay with? Did her city have a women's shelter? Maybe her church family would help her? "Please know that we believe no husband should hit his wife. We are praying for your safety and Stephen's!"

A week later, Leah messaged me again. This time she begged me to tell Jude not to hit her anymore. She threatened to call the police. "Why are people from America so rude?" she asked. She said he was even rude to Stephen and her family. She claimed Jude was "really, really crazy." Did our mother never teach Jude to be nice? she wondered.

Then she asked if Jude had always taken drugs. She'd never seen him like this before.

"Leave, Leah," I typed. "Take the baby and go somewhere safe."

Her answer was livid. She said Jude needed to leave, not her. This was her country, and she sponsored him.

Since making international calls was a challenge for Mom, I addressed the alleged domestic violence issue myself. When I told Jude of Leah's claims, he called her a drama queen. Not only that, he swore she had a relative who was a police officer. If he'd hit Leah, Jude claimed, the cop would've had him killed.

Because of all the wacky stuff he'd told me about Leah, I believed him. The way she hid his passport when it came time to renew his tourist visa. How she left the house every day with Stephen and drove to the local mall to "show off" to her friends, leaving him stranded at home. If her relative actually was a police officer, surely Leah would've reached out to him for help, wouldn't she?

I never heard from Leah again.

209

CHAPTER FORTY
The Plan

THE NEXT TIME I VISITED MOM SHE HANDED ME HER ADDRESS book. "We should call Leah's brother right now. We can tell him about Jude and Stephen, and he can have Leah call us."

I checked my watch. "It's the middle of the night there. I'll try later." I copied the address and phone number. "What if Leah won't leave him because of money, Mom? Do you want me to say we'll help her out financially? For the rest of her life?"

"Not yet. I would mention her talking to Stephen—being very quiet, very positive, telling him, 'Your daddy loves you.' Tell her to ask Stephen if his father has been touching his private parts. If so, she needs to tell him, 'Don't let him. It's not right.' She needs to teach him to tell her if it ever happens again."

"I have no idea if she knows or not," I said, "but I'm also going to tell her Jude abused me and Tom. That and the fact you saw something suspicious."

"It's liable to scare the you-know-what out of her."

"Yeah, but put yourself in her shoes. Wouldn't you want to hear the whole truth to know what you were dealing with?" Mom squeezed her eyes shut again and nodded. "Pedophilia is an illness,"

I told her. "Jude needs help. It would be great if he'd go to a psychologist and—"

Mom pursed her lips and shook her head. "There's no cure for pedophiles." I'd heard that too, and that the best solution is to keep pedophiles away from children.

"I think in time we should all write to Jude. To tell him we know everything and that we hate the things he's done. But not yet. Trey said not to tip off Jude until Leah knows what you saw. Describe that afternoon again for me." Mom turned away and didn't speak. What was she hiding? "I think you're blocking it out, Mom. Think about everything that happened that day. Was Jude often in the front bedroom?"

"Yes, because that's where all their stuff was." She pointed to the sleeper sofa where I sat. "But he slept out here, not in with them." I already knew that because Jude had complained to me that he tried to get the boys to sleep on the pullout couch with him, but they wouldn't.

"I'll try calling Leah's brother tonight," I told Mom before I left. "I'll let you know what happens."

Nothing happened. No matter how many times I dialed the number, no one ever answered.

Two days later, per Trey's suggestion, Chad drove down to meet with Detective Johnson, the officer in charge of crimes against children in my mother's county. He led Chad to a small room where he questioned him first about his conversation with Mom, then about Jude's history. At the end of their meeting, he asked if there was any way to get Mom in for an interview. Chad promised to try.

"My favorite thing he said was near the end when I apologized for bringing him this outlandish and convoluted story and probably causing him a bunch of work."

"'I've had a lot of stuff this week,' the detective said, 'but this is the most important item because it involves a crime against a child.'"

After Chad filled out a report form, he and Johnson reviewed the information line by line, then signed the bottom of the page.

Trey had warned me that in order for the blind side to be successful, we should not do or say anything to clue Jude in about what we were up to. Unfortunately, two days after Chad filed his police report, Mom blew the blind side.

Jude had called Mom from the South Pole. In the middle of Jude's discussion of his daily routine, Mom broke in. "Do not touch Stephen sexually ever again!"

Without a word, Jude hung up. That night, though, Mom's phone rang nonstop. She didn't pick up.

"He'll call back," I assured her the next day. "You know he will."

He did. "Leave me and Leah alone," Jude told Mom the next morning. "You'll never see me again. I'm not a monster. I didn't have kids to do this to them. You'll never find me."

Every hair on my body stiffened. Though he insisted he wasn't a monster, he sure sounded like one.

"He's going to run," I told Mom as she relayed the conversation. "I'd bet money on it."

Mom whimpered into the phone. "I'm never going to see my grandsons again."

After she hung up, I phoned Chad with the latest.

"Hardly the words of an innocent man," Chad said. Like me, he believed Jude would flee. "Maybe it wouldn't be a bad thing if Jude disappeared forever."

I woke the next morning distressed. How was I going to convince Mom to talk to Detective Johnson? Any day now, Jude's contract would end and he'd fly back to Southeast Asia to Leah and the boys. Then what?

When the phone rang in the middle of the morning, Mom's number lit up my caller ID screen and she began to leave a message. "Jude's friend Bill called yesterday." Bill was Jude's friend in Atlanta. Last summer, Jude, Leah, and the boys had stayed with him and his partner for nearly a month before driving north to Mom's.

I picked up the phone. "I'm here, Mom. What did Bill want?"

"He asked how I was, then he said the strangest thing. He said maybe he'd give you a call. Why would he call you? Have you ever met him?"

"Never," I said, my hand tightening on the receiver. "Is he in the habit of calling you?"

"He's only called me once or twice. This is all very strange."

"Plus it's the day after Jude said that 'I'm not a monster' stuff," I told her. "Jude put him up to this. What do you want to bet? They're testing you, Mom, trying to figure out your next move." And they wanted to call me to figure out if Mom had spread the news of Jude's abuse of Stephen.

After I hung up with Mom, I logged on to my computer. Bill wasn't my Facebook friend, but I might be able to see his wall via Jude's. There he was. I scrolled through his photos and stopped at a picture of Will. In the photo, adorable, doll-like Will sat in front of a computer. On the screen was a woman who appeared to be lying belly down on a bed, with her tongue lolling out of her mouth. She wore an animal print bathing suit or lingerie. I scanned the rest of his pictures but didn't find anything else of note.

I returned to Jude's page. In the top-left corner, I clicked on the link to his employer, then copied and pasted the web address into an email to myself. I might need to contact his boss someday.

I checked Leah's Facebook wall as well. Paging down, I came across two social media images. The first said, "A real man never hurts a woman. Be careful when you make a woman cry because

God counts her tears." Leah's asking for help, I thought. Which means she'd told the truth all those months ago.

The other meme pictured a boy cowering on a sofa. A man's hand holding a belt appeared on the side of the image. The headline read "Like if you hate child abuse. Share if you want to stop child abuse." To me, it seemed Leah was definitely trying to send a message to someone. I emailed the two images to Chad, Tom, and myself.

After lunch that day, Detective Johnson called me. "Listen, I can't close this case until I have an eyewitness statement from your mother. I need to talk to her. Can you get her to come in? Or should I go to her house?"

"Oh good Lord, no," I told him. "She'd have a cow if you parked your cruiser in her driveway and the neighbors saw. I'll bring her to you."

"No," Mom said moments later when I phoned her. "I won't do it. I won't make things worse." When I protested, she wouldn't budge. She kept saying, "Absolutely not."

Devastated, I spent the rest of the afternoon trying to come up with a way to persuade Mom to change her mind.

CHAPTER FORTY-ONE
Prayer Works

THAT NIGHT AFTER SUPPER, I DROPPED WYATT AT HIS KARATE CLASS and navigated the slushy distance to our small group Bible study. Exhausted by a long day's work in his very chilly warehouse, Chad begged off. Leaving behind the lights of downtown, I traveled the steep central hill of the neighborhood, bearing left halfway up to head toward our friends' house.

Due to the bitter cold and marginal road conditions, attendance at our small group was sparse. That night during the discussion, my mind kept leaping ahead, planning what to tell the group when it was time for prayer requests. All evening my secret rested inside me, heavy. Even so, I believed as soon as I asked friends to pray, my family's issues would begin to lose their power.

When the group facilitator asked for prayer requests, I raised my hand. "I'm going to share what's going on in my family. It's pretty awful, and I apologize for that, but if I can't tell you all, who can I tell?"

Glancing from face to face as I presented my family's story, I watched emotions flicker: discomfort, compassion, concern. When I finished, I gave the group something specific to pray for. "Besides protection for the boys and Leah, please pray my mom will go to the police with me on Saturday. I'm calling her first thing tomorrow."

The next morning after Wyatt left for school, I jotted down a list of reasons Mom should talk to the police. If I provided four or five, perhaps she'd agree to supply a witness statement. To protect Stephen and Will from Jude's sexual advances. To protect other kids from Jude's sexual advances. To get help for Jude. And Leah. To do the right thing.

When Mom answered the phone, I told her Detective Johnson had contacted me again. "Mom, he needs resolution in this case, and in order for that to happen, you have to—"

"Fine. Yes. I'll talk to him."

The day before our meeting with Detective Johnson, I drove to Mom's house to spend the night. We went out to dinner then watched *The Waltons* before turning in. Sitting on the edge of the guest bed to text Chad good night, I shivered. The abuse happened in this room.

At 7:20 the next morning, Mom tapped on my door. "Time to get up."

Peering between the slats of the blinds, I groaned. Snow blanketed the world. I wondered if there was ice beneath the snow. If so, walking Mom out to the car, driving down the steep hill out of her development, and traveling to the police station would prove a challenge.

I dressed quickly, pulling on brown corduroys and a peach sequined top. I stepped into shiny ballet flats and ran a narrow belt through my belt loops. After I applied makeup, I slipped on my rings, then my watch. I wanted to appear put together, not desperate.

In the living room, my mother waited in her lavender recliner with her cat, Rosie, dozing on her lap. Mom wore gray slacks and a cranberry sweater over a turtleneck. Her white hair framed her round face in soft curls. I knew the hair in back was probably pillow flat because she usually forgot to fluff it, but no doubt I'd be the only one to notice.

At the dining room table, we ate our cereal in silence. The woods beyond her deck were frosted and lovely.

"Stephen was naked when I walked into the guest bedroom. Jude's hands were, you know, down there and—" Instead of looking at me, she stared into her cereal bowl.

I gently gripped her wrist. "Stop. Save it for the detective. I only want you to have to tell the story once."

When Detective Johnson opened the side door to the police station, I stepped back. He filled the entire doorframe. With his head shaved and blonde lashes and brows, his face was deceptively bland. Immediately, I sensed his trustworthiness, and when he steadied Mom with his oversized hands, I knew he was kind. At his side, tucked into its holster, a pistol was the only clue that he was more than a former college defensive lineman or someone's big brother.

Detective Johnson posed his questions to Mom. Tell me about yourself. What did you see that day? What was Jude like growing up? Were there other incidents of a sexual nature?

In the small examination room, Mom sat up straight, appeared alert, and was articulate. She answered each question carefully.

Detective Johnson slid a form across the table to Mom. He asked her to write down everything she told him, especially what she saw happen between Jude and Stephen. When she finished, she needed to sign the bottom of the page and date it. Mom asked if I could write the report and then she would sign it. Johnson said that would be fine, and left the room.

"What will happen now?" I asked when he returned.

217

Before answering, he skimmed over the words I'd written. "Now that this report is filed, warn his wife."

Mom and I had debated whether or not Leah knew Jude was abusing Stephen. I told the detective how in a private Facebook message Jude had bemoaned the wrecked status of his marriage and family life.

"He told me how he and Leah—that's his wife—hardly ever sleep together. He shared that with me and Mom. What guy discusses his sex life with his mother and sister? Oh, and he bragged to our brother Tom that he can still, at fifty-something, have sex four times in twenty-four hours. He has no boundaries. None. Leah insists on sleeping with the boys and she leaves the house every morning with Stephen. They stay away all day. My guess is she's trying to protect Stephen. She probably thinks since Will is so young, Jude won't mess with him."

Echoing my earlier question, Mom asked what would happen now. On the table, Johnson laced his fingers and sighed. "With him being out of the country, this is tough. I don't have the budget to go after him at the South Pole, but when you get word that he's coming back to West Virginia—" I broke in to assure the detective that we would probably never see Jude again. If Jude returned to the States at all, he'd probably head for Colorado, California, or Atlanta to stay with his friend Bill.

"Well, if you hear he's coming back to the States at all, let me know," Johnson said. "I'll get the funding and go after him." The way his eyes became flinty told me he would relish the hunt.

"Will he be arrested if he comes back?" Mom wanted to know.

"Can't say for sure. I do know he'll be brought in for questioning. Who knows what will happen after that? I'll add this form and some of my own comments to the file, then unfortunately, it'll be considered a cold case unless he returns home."

Back at Mom's house, we tried again to reach Leah's brother by phone. No one picked up. There wasn't an answering machine either. I promised Mom I'd continue to call. It was the weekend. Maybe they were out on the town.

That night I called both numbers twice, thirty minutes apart, but still no one answered. The next morning, I phoned again, to no avail. Desperate to contact Leah, I sent her a private Facebook message. I prayed Jude did not know her password.

> *Hello Leah:*
>
> *I hope you and the boys are doing well. I am writing to you at Mom's request. For the past few days I have tried to call both telephone numbers Mom has for you. No one answered and that's why I'm writing you here.*
>
> *Mom (Jean) thinks it would be in Stephen and Will's best interest if you did not leave either of them alone with Jude.*
>
> *When the four of you visited the United States last summer, Mom witnessed Jude sexually abusing Stephen in the front bedroom.*
>
> *Over the years, Jude has had problems with sex. In fact, he sexually abused me for years, as well as our brother Tom. There were other incidents as well.*
>
> *We hoped that he no longer had these deviant behaviors, but we know now we were wrong. We are appalled and deeply saddened that he would use Stephen for his own sexual gratification.*
>
> *We are so sorry this is happening. We are very concerned for you and the boys. We hope you know someone who can help you three.*
>
> *At some point Jude mentioned that you have a relative who is a police officer, a brother or uncle maybe? Perhaps this person can help protect you and the boys. This must stop. It is*

very sick behavior. The boys should not grow up thinking this is acceptable.

If there is any way we can help from here, please let us know. Again, we are so sorry for this very difficult situation.

Love,

Dina, your sister-in-law

CHAPTER FORTY-TWO
FedEx

Since Mark's wife Valerie was battling cancer, we kept the news about Jude from her and Mark for as long as possible. Finally, Mom phoned Mark to fill him in. Moments later, he texted me asking for details, so I called him. He listened without comment as I reviewed the details. Afterward, he thanked me for what Chad and I had accomplished to date and promised to pray for the problem.

Due to her illness, I wasn't sure if Mark would tell his wife or not, but the next morning on Valerie's Facebook page, there was a cryptic post: "I have an unspoken prayer request of a breakthrough that needs to be answered soon. I know God is able. Praying and fasting for it."

Less than twenty-four hours later, Jude gave her post a thumbs up.

Each morning and night I phoned Leah's brother in Southeast Asia. I always let the phone ring at least eight times. No one ever answered.

Any day now Jude would be back with his family, with access to his young sons. I went back through my emails and Facebook messages to see if he had mentioned a travel date. On a whim, I texted Mark to see what he knew. He thought he remembered an email where Jude mentioned returning to his family on February 21. That was nearly a month away. I had three whole weeks to come up with a plan.

I decided to FedEx Leah a letter. That way someone had to sign for it. I also enclosed a copy for Leah's brother, in case Jude found and destroyed Leah's. In addition, I included contact information for a children's advocacy resource in Leah's country.

On January 30, I drove to the FedEx dispatch center to send the packet. The clerk handed me the receipt, pointing to the web address where I could track the package. She said it would arrive on February 3, was that okay? I nodded. Leah and her brother would receive the packet eighteen days before Jude's return.

The morning of February 3, I checked the FedEx website. Someone named Damien signed for the package. Grinning, I leaned back in my desk chair. I did it! I got the information from West Virginia to Southeast Asia. Now the question was, would this Damien person open the package and give Leah her envelope, and her brother his?

That night, when I heard nothing from either of them, I dialed both their phone numbers multiple times. Per usual, no one answered.

After Wyatt left for school the next morning, I checked email. When Jude's name appeared in my inbox, I gawked. It didn't happen often, Jude emailing me. Usually he sent messages via Facebook, and even those were rare. Jude sent this email to me, both of my brothers, and our cousin Ellen.

There were photographs attached to the email. The first showed Stephen and Will, in matching bright blue shirts, being pushed in a wheelbarrow. The second picture featured a close-up of Will, his hair mussed, his liquid eyes so dark, you couldn't see the pupils.

The photo I studied the longest was a group shot taken in front of a trio of crucifixes with Jesus in the middle. Near the memorial,

Jude's family posed in two rows. The two boys stood in front; the six adults behind. What interested me most was how Jude had typed everyone's name and relational title beneath the photograph. Leah stood between her brother and mother. There were also two aunts and a cousin.

I leaned closer to the screen. Was this the brother I sent the FedEx package to? But the name Jude typed for him was not the name written in Mom's address book. Then I had a thought. What if this brother was on Facebook?

In another tab, I opened Facebook and typed in this brother's name: Arto Franklin. There he was. He and I shared two mutual Facebook friends—Leah and Jude. Without hesitation I sent him a friend request and sat back to wait.

Within the hour, Arto accepted my request.

"Hello," I typed. "I am Jude's sister, Leah's sister-in-law. Thank you for accepting my friend request. I recently sent a large envelope to Leah. Do you know if she received it?"

He replied that yes, once he signed for the package, he gave it to Leah. My mouth fell open as I stared at the screen. Arto had given my letter to Leah. Plus, since he knew English, I now had a way to communicate with her.

"Did Leah give you a smaller envelope," I typed, "one that was inside the larger one?"

When Arto typed no, I frowned. I thought surely Leah would read her letter as soon as she received it, then give her brother his envelope, which he would read immediately. Right away, they'd discuss the contents and decide what to do. But that didn't happen. Did Leah take the package home without even opening it? Time for a new plan.

"I have something to tell you about Leah and Jude," I typed, "but it is unpleasant. Are you willing to get involved?" He asked if the issue would make Jude mad. At my desk I shook my head. So

Arto was familiar with Jude's temper. I replied yes, it would definitely make Jude mad.

A few moments later, his answer appeared. "I want to help."

"Send me your email address."

Once he complied, I emailed Arto the documents I'd sent Leah by FedEx: a cover letter to him, the letter to Leah (essentially, the Facebook message I'd recently sent her), and a page with telephone numbers—mine, Mom's, Chad's, that of a child advocacy center.

Within ten minutes Arto's response arrived. "OMG. Is this true?" I'm afraid so, I told him. He vowed to protect the boys and get help for Jude as well. He then asked me to pray for Jude and Leah, and for the boys to be okay.

I studied his words. He was going to get help for Jude? He wanted me to pray for Jude and Leah and the nephews? I felt unexpected hope.

For an hour we messaged back and forth. He said he would gather himself, his (and Leah's) mother, their mother's second husband (a policeman), and Jude to discuss the situation. His plan sounded like an intervention. "That's a fantastic idea," I told him.

Arto asked what else his family should do. I said I believed it would be wise to move Leah and the boys away from Jude. Might Leah's mother allow her to return home?

"Surely it is possible," Arto answered.

It was midnight United States time when he signed off. In closing, he promised to report back soon, then he thanked me for my kindness and said, "God bless."

CHAPTER FORTY-THREE
Research

The following Monday, I sent Leah a short email. She did not reply. She probably mistrusted me because I hadn't helped her the first time she asked. There was no word from Arto, either. However, something he'd said a few days prior poked at me, the thing about getting help for Jude. If I truly loved my brother, I should want that too, right? So I began to Google.

I read about the difference between pedophilia and pedosexuality. Pedophilia describes a sexual preference, not a sexual behavior. Persons with pedophilia fantasize about prepubescent children, respond sexually toward them, and wish to have social interactions and contact with them. A pedosexual, though, is an individual who acts on their urges.

A health newsletter from Harvard said, "There is no cure, so the focus is on protecting children." The article estimated that "about 50 to 70 percent of people with pedophilic tendencies are also diagnosed with another paraphilia, such as exhibitionism, voyeurism, or sadism." I'd personally experienced Jude's exhibitionism and voyeurism, and to me, his frequent beatings of Tom spoke of his sadism.

The newsletter also stated that "most people with pedophilic tendencies eventually act on their sexual urges in some way. Typically, this involves exposing themselves to children, watching naked children, masturbating in front of children, or touching children's genitals."[1]

This explained so much. All along, when Mom insisted she only saw Jude touch Stephen "down there," I believed she was protecting Jude by downplaying the abuse, or maybe she was blocking out what she saw. Surely there'd been more than just touching. But this article supported her account. It also explained what happened to me.

For years, I didn't want to tell anyone the specifics of my abuse. The details didn't seem vile enough. But during my research that day, I found the website for the Rape, Abuse, and Incest National Network (RAINN) and their definition of rape: "Penetration, no matter how slight, of the vagina or anus with any body part or object, or oral penetration of a sex organ of another person, without the consent of the victim."[2]

As I read those words, my eyes spilled over. I was raped, not by a penis, but by fingers.

For decades I'd believed that Jude didn't rape me because I thought rape had to include penile penetration. My experience mostly involved Jude's fingers inside me. I clenched my thighs to stop the sensations—probing, wriggling. Millipedes.

All my life I've compared my abuse story to every other abuse story I hear. At least it wasn't my birth father who violated me. It was just my brother. I wasn't raped with a Coke bottle, just my brother's fingers. I had so much less to complain about, didn't I?

During the interview with Detective Johnson, he'd asked me to describe what Jude did to me. I'd glanced at my mother. I hesitated to answer with her in the room.

I wanted Mom to believe that nightly Jude climbed on me and rode me wild while I wept and fought. I didn't want her to know my abuse was actually a quiet, furtive thing. Jude kneeling next to my bed, his roving hands beneath my quilt, then under the ruffled hem of my plaid flannel nightgown from Sears and Roebuck while I pretended to be asleep. Or frozen. Dead.

What satisfaction could be gained by touching someone seemingly without life—a mannequin, a corpse? And if while I pretended to be sound asleep, I allowed my mind to travel somewhere else—next door to the McCallisters, downtown to the police station to file a report—what harm was he doing really?

When I told Chad about the meeting with Detective Johnson, I confessed how I thought maybe what happened to me wasn't all that bad. Other people experienced so much worse, right?

Chad drew me close and spoke into my hair. "What Jude did to you was wrong. Wrong. Wrong. Wrong."

As I continued to delve into the topic of sexual dysfunction, searching all the pertinent phrases I could think of, I found an essay in *The Atlantic* written by a man sexually attracted to young children called "I, Pedophile." The reaction of the writer's loved ones challenged me: "My family and friends stood by since my arrest and love and accept me, despite my sexual flaws."[3]

His statement brought to mind the Golden Rule, which says you should do unto others as you would have them do unto you. If I were Jude, afflicted with pedophilia, what would I want from others, from my family? Surely I would crave their compassion, maybe even their assistance. Unflinching support. What I wouldn't want was for my family members to loathe and abandon me because of my sickness, repugnant though it was.

What if I offered to help Jude get treatment so he could be a good father and husband? It would be so beautiful if he found restoration. Did I possess that sort of mercy? Even if I did, would Jude accept my help? But realistically speaking, how could I accomplish that from half a world away?

In tandem with the "I, Pedophile" essay, *The Atlantic* ran an interview with James Cantor, PhD, an international expert on pedophilia.[4] Cantor stated, "The best current evidence suggests that pedophilia results from atypical wiring in the brain. This field of research is still very new, but it appears that there exists what could be considered a 'cross-wiring' in the brain anatomy that is responsible for controlling natural social instincts or behavior. Although learning happens after birth, humans are pre-wired to recognize and respond to certain stimuli. It seems, from research conducted thus far, that stimuli that usually elicits nurturing and protective responses in most adults are instead eliciting sexual responses in pedophiles."

When Alice Dreger, the interviewer, asked Cantor, "So are pedophiles 'born that way?'" he offered the following explanation. "In studies, pedophiles show signs that their sexual interests are related to brain structure and that at least some differences existed in their brains before birth." This disputed the theory held by Tom and me, as well as by every counselor I'd spoken with about Jude: that he abused because he'd been abused. If Cantor's research was correct, no abuser "made" Jude a pedophile. He was born that way.

Cantor went on to say that "pedophiles are the most likely to commit their offenses when they feel that they have nothing going for them in their lives and that therefore they have nothing to lose. People are most likely to do the most desperate things when they feel the most desperate. Unfortunately, much of the current social systems greatly increase rather than decrease these people's feelings of desperation."

Cantor's detailing of a risky setting for a pedophile sounded remarkably similar to Jude's own description of his life with Leah and the boys.

Another journal article I read on father–son incest, written by Mark Williams, PhD, noted, "Several cases have been reported in which sexual contact between father and son occurred in an apparently disorganized family situation in which impulsive, physically abusive behavior by the father was the norm. These fathers were exploitatively involved with their families, usually pansexual in orientation and often sexually abused both sons and daughters. The age of the sons at point of initial sexual contact was usually prepubertal."[5]

Immediately I recalled an old private Facebook message from Jude in which he complained that Leah was getting more controlling. Several times she'd told him to leave. She'd torn up his immigration papers. Tried to bait Jude into hitting her. She threatened to take him to court for battery, even though Jude swore there was no evidence of physical abuse. In fact, he claimed Leah had threatened him with a knife in their bedroom.

To me, Jude's family environment definitely seemed like the kind of circumstance Williams described as being at risk for father–son sexual abuse.

Other scenarios Williams described could also have been lifted from Jude's life. Dr. Williams wrote about another case study of father–son sexual abuse. "He (the abusing father) explains his long-standing sexual relationship with his son to be a consequence of the poor sexual relationship with his wife."

I wondered if Jude's lack of sexual intimacy with Leah drove him to abuse Stephen. Or was it vice versa?

The article also stated: "Two reports of father–son incest indicate that in extremely disorganized families in which psychosis is present in one or more family members, incestuous behavior may become part of the family's interactional pattern."

Though Jude didn't have an official diagnosis that I was aware of, Mom, with lived experience, and Aunt Mae, who worked as a psychiatric nurse for decades, both believed Jude to be bipolar. In addition, my counselor friend Trey believed Jude to be mentally ill on multiple levels. In addition, I remembered how years ago, Jude had shared that he'd been diagnosed with seasonal affective disorder (SAD). I learned that SAD is a subtype of bipolar disorder.

In his journal article, Dr. Williams quoted another researcher, A. Taubman, who also provided analyses of incestuous families. "Incestuous fathers, for example, are often either authoritarian, dependent, infantile, or generally irresponsible. Mothers in incestuous families often are either weak and submissive, frigid, promiscuous, or indifferent to the needs of others."

As a father, Jude swung between those extremes. According to Leah, he beat her and demanded she respect and obey him. Other times he whined that she left him trapped at home with no food. One time he claimed he was surviving by eating only mangos from the tree in their yard and eggs.

During my research, I also learned about imprinting. Proponents of the imprinting theory believe that when a child reaches the age of sexual awakening or curiosity, the thing of a sexual nature they see initially can become a long-term source of arousal for the person, possibly for life. When I read that, I recalled the paperback book in my mother's dresser drawer. In that story, the victim had been a young girl. Mark and Tom also spoke of pornography magazines. What images did my three brothers see on those pages?

CHAPTER FORTY-FOUR
Daddy's Home

LATER THAT NIGHT, I CHECKED MY WATCH. IN APPROXIMATELY twenty-four hours, Jude would be back home with his family. No doubt he was in an airport now, waiting for his final flight out.

As I imagined Leah's stress over Jude's impending homecoming, everything in me felt stretched tight. I remembered the time Jude returned home from college, and how afraid I'd been, certain the abuse would resume. Was that how Leah was feeling now that her four-month respite from her unstable husband was nearly over?

An hour later my phone vibrated with a Facebook notification. From Jude. He messaged me he was on a layover in Christchurch, New Zealand, on his way home. He'd recently changed the pin number on his debit card, and the bank had mailed the new number to Mom's house. He asked me to call her for the number then send it back to him.

It felt strange communicating with Jude, pretending nothing unusual was going on, like I didn't know his awful secret, as if I hadn't sent an incriminating letter to his wife and her brother.

I called Mom, but she hadn't received anything from Jude's credit card company. She did have mail from the state of Colorado for him, though. I messaged Jude the info.

Jude thanked me, asked about the weather, then signed off, saying he'd be leaving New Zealand for Southeast Asia at 8:30 that night.

I exited Facebook and Googled how long his flight would take —approximately twelve hours. In bed, my mind whirled. I hadn't heard from Arto recently and hadn't heard from Leah in ages. What if they decided to do nothing about Jude? What if Leah thought she had to stay with him in order to provide for the boys?

I threw back the covers, crept over to my desk, and composed an email.

> *Dear Leah and/or Arto:*
>
> *It's me, Dina, in America. I'm very sorry to email you this late at night but I want to tell you two things before Jude returns.*
>
> *1. Leah, I am very sorry that I did not listen to you a few years ago when you told me Jude was hurting you. I was wrong to believe him, not you. I wish I had done more to help you then.*
>
> *Please forgive me.*
>
> *2. Leah, I do NOT want you to stay with Jude for the sake of financial security. I very much want you and the boys to have a safe life without him. If anything happens and you find yourself in a position without money to live, please let me know.*
>
> *Chad and I are willing to provide your living expenses. We want the best for you three.*

I didn't consult anyone about my offer of financial help because I believed my family would balk at providing support for Leah and the boys. They'd worry about her taking advantage of us. Since the cost of living was so much lower in Leah's country, it would not be an expensive endeavor. Chad and I could pay for it, if necessary.

It was a moot point though. Neither Leah nor Arto answered my email.

Three days later a Facebook message from Arto came through. Leah and Arto's mother and all of the "elders" had decided that if Jude abused one of the boys again, they would take him to the local police station and the U.S. embassy.

So they'd decided against an intervention, I thought. Still, their new plan wasn't awful. I asked Arto if Leah had received my recent email. He said since she didn't have a nanny, she was too busy with the boys to check email. He also said he hoped his family had made a wise conclusion. In closing, he urged me to pray for the boys and Leah. He hoped God would work in the situation.

At least the elders were aware of the dilemma now, I thought. If nothing else, it meant more eyes to watch Jude. The only thing was, I remembered Jude saying he and Leah lived in the city and her family lived thirty minutes away in the country. How then could the family monitor Jude?

The following day Arto sent another message letting me know that Jude had returned home and the family was ready and watching the boys. Again he urged me to pray that God would change Jude's attitude and help him get "better and better."

"Thank you very much for this information, Arto," I typed. "My family is very grateful for what you are doing. We are praying very hard that Jude will be a good husband and father."

Arto said God's will would be done. And that he'd be in touch if anything bad happened.

CHAPTER FORTY-FIVE
Spies

Though I stewed a bit over the Jude problem, for the most part, I experienced peace. I pondered the saying "All it takes for evil to flourish is for good men to do nothing." I decided the quote didn't apply to me. I had done something, and as I saw it, there wasn't much more I could do.

A month later, in an email exchange with April—a writer friend of mine who knew about my childhood trauma—I mentioned Jude was at it again, abusing children, this time his own.

"You know my fiancé Ethan works for a security agency within the federal government, right? I bet he'd give you advice."

I read her words again. If April's fiancé got involved, it could change everything.

The day after I gave Ethan permission to investigate Jude and his family, he located information on Jude, Leah, and the boys: where they lived, their social security numbers, and so on. I was amazed and terrified. What had I set in motion?

Based on the information I provided, Ethan assured me the facts were sufficient to warrant an investigation. He was stationed in the States now, but he knew people working in the country where Jude and Leah lived. They would pursue the matter.

I imagined operatives in head-to-toe black surrounding Jude and Leah's house at night, watching Jude through his windows the way he'd watched me years ago. Back then, tucked within midnight shadows, he thought I couldn't see him. But inside the brick skin of our home, I was always aware of his presence and his need.

I didn't tell Mom or Mark about Ethan, but in time, I shared the information with Tom. He was so consumed by our family's quandary, I hoped the news might buoy his mood.

The update made Tom giddy. He fantasized how the confrontation might play out. Through visual surveillance or via listening equipment, when Ethan's friends collected the last bit of evidence needed to arrest Jude, would they break down the front door and grab him or whisk him into an unmarked car as he strolled home from the market?

I tried to picture Jude's facial expression when they apprehended him. Would it be one of horror or relief? Perhaps part of him was weary of pretending. Surely there would be fear. Fear of everyone knowing what he was. Fear of prison.

Tom and I discussed what Jude's incarceration might entail. Would life as a convicted sexual offender in Southeast Asia be as frightening as it is reported to be in America? Every jailed child sexual offender I'd ever read about had to be moved to a protective area of a prison, away from the vigilante justice of the other inmates.

Jude wasn't a tall man, and in numerous shirtless photos on Facebook, his collarbones and ribs pressed against his skin. Now in his late fifties, he'd be easy to bully.

Despite my commitment to protect my nephews and get help for Jude, anger often ambushed me. Why hadn't he changed? Didn't my decades of shunning accomplish anything?

What would Jude think when he figured out that Chad and I were the ones who filed a police report against him? As far as I knew, he had no idea anyone but Mom knew of his crime. Would he hate her for telling us? Would he despise Chad and me for contacting law enforcement?

Even though I knew we were doing the right thing, I felt conflicted. For comfort, I reminded myself of April's words. "One day those little boys will be so thankful someone fought for them." Even so, I was afraid. Scared he would attack Mom's credibility. Or mine.

I felt both tired and ashamed of my fear, and more than ready to be rid of it.

One day, it occurred to me I wasn't the only fearful member of our family. Fear ruled all of us. Fear of financial insecurity, though we have always had more than enough. Fear of what others think of us.

Once I spent an entire day writing about it, shaping and editing my words for hours.

"Fear is the garment, the covering we wear, my family and me. Fear is like my father's World War II blanket folded sloppily in a basement cabinet: ugly brown—dirt mixed with bad coffee. The cloth will never lose the stains of war, of what it has seen and experienced. It has seldom known sunlight, rarely felt open air.

"It is gratifying to watch my mother lift a corner of the blanket. Finally. She didn't raise it for me or Tom, but now she does for her grandsons. She sees a greater sin and is ready to suffer the results of the bringing of light. Or perhaps she is simply old, and weary of folding and refolding the same wretched, rough fabric.

"Watching her struggle with its heft, I offer assistance. As we pinch corners and step together and apart, as Mom reveals more, then amends those revelations, I'm unsure what the complete truth is. I realize I may never know the entire truth as long as there are individuals who hog the blanket, who hug it, not minding its dank odor, who mistake its pressing weight for comfort. This blanket has never known a time without war."

I also wrote Jude a letter, one I would never send:

There was a time I believed Mick Jagger correct when he sang it was a drag to get old. Now though, I welcome the advance of years. The beauty of aging is in the knowing: yourself, others, truth.

I know now that I live in light—a morning glory, face to the sun. You exist in darkness—a fungus, pleated and moist. I embrace love. You fear it, flee it. You trust in silence. I speak now. For decades I had no voice. Now I speak on behalf of the voiceless.

At last I understand you, can lift a flap of your skin and see inside—the throbbing, the instinct. I recognize how again, again, you become the father of lies. You believe them. You speak them: "I love my family. I am not a monster. My transgressions will never be known."

I don't hate you. I pity you. My flesh recoils at the memory of your compulsion, addictions, rage. All those years ago I said you needed to love yourself. I see now why it is impossible. Your hell will be a mirror.

You long to return to this country, this state, this family, but we do not want you here. You hate wherever you are, introduce poison wherever you go. Here is your mirror. You are the America you despise—the one where the powerful take what they want, what they think is rightfully theirs, from the least of these. You are your current hiding place—too hot, crawling with corruption, toxic with pollution.

Eventually you will leave there. You always do. You are Cain, doomed to wander the world, a vagrant. Unknown, unloved, alone.

I was trapped in my dilemma: wanting to help Jude, but also wanting him to pay for his crimes against me, Tom, Stephen, and God only knows who else.

For a long time, that's how I gauged the quality of my day, the quality of me. If I desired strongly to help Jude exorcise his obsession, that was a good day. I was a good person. If I felt the old fury bubble up and hoped he'd be assaulted daily in prison, that was a bad day and I was a horrible human.

CHAPTER FORTY SIX
Mark Speaks

MY BROTHER TOM WOULD NOT RELINQUISH THE THEORY THAT someone made Jude a pedophile, who in time became a sexual predator. In fact, Tom was nearly 100 percent convinced it was our dad. I disagreed. My belief that our father was not a lecherous man hinged on the fact that Dad was circumspect when he bathed me. Not once did he touch me inappropriately while I was in the tub.

From his seat on the commode, Dad gave instructions. "Get the washcloth wet, Honey Pot. Now rub the soap on it. Scrub down there. Make it clean." Then he'd pivot away from me to face the door. "Be sure and rinse it good. It's a sensitive area."

I shared the memory with Tom, but it didn't change his mind. I also told him about my research, the various theories on pedophilia. He didn't care. Since he believed Jude's negative influence was Dad, the only person left to question was Mark, so on the morning of March 16, 2015, I emailed him.

> Dear Mark:
> I want you to know that nothing you say at this point will surprise, shock, or offend me. Nor will I hold anything against you. The past is what it is. God allowed it. I survived it. I have

experienced healing from it. I rejoice and claim Psalm 30:10–12 over my life. "You turned my wailing into dancing; you removed my sackcloth and clothed me with joy, that my heart may sing your praises and not be silent."

Currently I am like part of a family who experienced the loss of a relation due to mysterious circumstances. I want to gather all the facts and evidence I can to make sense of it all, in order to have closure.

I am like an adopted child now grown and seeking answers to the questions surrounding my early years. I am trying to answer the question why. This is the reason I want to know what you know, all of it.

Love,

Dina

P.S. Ephesians 5:11 says, "Have nothing to do with the fruitless deeds of darkness, but rather expose them."

I hoped my liberal use of scripture would sway my oldest brother.

Mark called immediately. I headed for the kitchen, where my list of questions lay on the table. To begin the conversation, I presented one of Mom's theories. There'd been an odd man in the neighborhood. Had he molested Jude or Mark, or both?

Mark chuckled. "No. That guy was harmless, schizophrenic maybe, but not a pervert."

"How old were you when you demanded to leave the boy bedroom?"

"Thirteen or fourteen."

"Why did you move out? Did you see Jude do something to Tom?"

Mark answered quickly—too quickly in my opinion—saying by the grace of God he remembered nothing inappropriate.

"Then what made you insist on moving out? What caused that extreme of a response in you?"

"Because Jude was a homo sapien!"

"A what?"

"A homo sapien!" Mark's voice cracked like a juvenile boy's.

"Are you talking about our code word for gay people when we were growing up?" I asked. Mark didn't respond. "Is it possible you saw Jude headed that way and it made you uncomfortable and that's why you demanded to move out?"

"I think it's logical to assume that." Mark's voice sounded grown-up again, like Spock's on *Star Trek*.

"Mom told me Jude abused Tom multiple times. But you never saw anything?"

"Nothing."

"Then what or who turned Jude into a child molester?"

"There was porn in the house."

"I know that, Mark. We've discussed this before." My fingernails cut into my palms as I tried to keep my voice calm.

The words he spoke next spilled out like oil, coating everything. "Some of it was pedophilic in nature."

My head struck the wall behind me. There was child pornography in our house? Besides the smutty graphic novel I knew about? Magazines with photographs of real kids, not just drawings?

Saliva pooled in my mouth. My stomach heaved. Did the pornography belong to Jude? Or Mom? Or Dad? Or to both of them? Revulsion filled me. My family is so dirty! Inside my mind the word *dirty* sounded childlike, but it was true. We were filthy, vulgar.

But then I had a thought. "This actually makes sense," I said. I went on to tell Mark about the concept of imprinting I'd found during my research. "If Jude was becoming sexually curious and he found or procured that kind of pornography, or someone gave it to him …" My voice trailed off as I pictured Jude, a cute little boy with round blue eyes, huddled over images of naked children, titillated by the newness of it all. The possibility. "That would explain what he did to Tom and me. And Stephen."

Mark suddenly began to apologize for the past. Again. "You don't have to do this," I said. "You apologized a long time ago, the night before Dad's memorial service, remember?"

Mark spoke slowly. "What do you think I'm apologizing for?"

"Honestly, I'm not a hundred percent sure."

"I'm talking about that one time in the car, in the back seat. My foot brushed your crotch. And another time, I accidentally touched your breast. Not on purpose though."

I almost laughed. My sweet, righteous big brother was apologizing for accidents.

"I don't remember either of those things, so don't worry about them. You're a good man—a good husband and father."

Still, he didn't sound okay when he said goodbye. Perhaps he thought he'd said too much, and in doing so, betrayed our family.

A month or so later, at my prompting, Tom called Mark. Mark and his wife had recently moved over a thousand miles to be closer to their son, daughter-in-law, and grandchildren. "Mark probably needs someone to talk to," I told Tom, "another man, someone he knows."

Tom let me know whenever he spoke to Mark. Sometimes they reminisced. Other times they prayed together. To me, it was beautiful. For years they'd hardly spoken, now this. But then one night, the reparation of their relationship ended abruptly.

Tom pressured Mark to join our blind side of Jude. Mark refused. He said he would not lie. If Jude ever brought up the subject, Mark planned to tell him everything: that we all knew about his abuse of Stephen, and that I'd sent a letter to Leah and her brother. Mark's refusal to side with us infuriated Tom. Their brief reconciliation sputtered and died.

Panicked by the possibility of Mark exposing the plan to protect Jude's boys, at our next home group meeting, I solicited prayer again. "Please pray Mark will not tell Jude anything."

A few nights later, Mark called me to express how much he appreciated all Chad and I had done to safeguard Jude's boys. He assured me if Jude contacted him, he would not reveal the steps we'd taken. "If he starts asking questions, I'll call you and Chad to find out how you want me to proceed."

CHAPTER FORTY-SEVEN
The Aftermath

FOR A WHILE THERE, AS OUR FAMILY WAITED FOR NEWS AS TO whether or not Jude had been caught in an abusive act and taken away—meaning that the boys and Leah were safe—I felt like Dad. My computer was my ham radio setup where I received news from the other side of the world then disseminated it to the appropriate parties. Or not.

On the other side of the world, Leah stayed silent. And her brother Arto kept quiet as well. Part of that was my fault. A month or so after Jude returned home, Arto reached out to me once more via Facebook Messenger. Not with news of the boys, not with prayers for Jude's healing, but with a request for money. Actually, the request felt more like a demand, and the amount was significant. Chad and I agreed that accommodating the request might lead to a never-ending stream of pleas, so we said no. Soon after, Arto unfriended me on Facebook. Once that happened, I stopped checking Facebook daily, hoping for an update regarding Jude's household.

Besides, whether or not Chad and I supplied money to Arto, the chances of him observing anything alarming and taking action were slim if Jude was correct and he and Leah lived thirty miles from her family. Still, given Leah's extreme dislike, possibly even hatred, of Jude, I thought perhaps she'd work with Arto to rid her home of her odious husband.

What did she even think of my tell-all letter? I wondered. I guessed I would never find out. There had been no communication between us since the night I apologized to her and offered financial support. Even so, I kept all of her messages to me, along with my responses, in our shared Facebook Messenger thread. I also copied and pasted them into a separate document, thinking Jude would erase all of our conversations, but he never did, leading me to believe Leah never gave him her log-in information. After posting the two memes I'd seen in the spring of 2014, Leah never posted on her Facebook page again.

With Arto in a huff, my family and I resigned ourselves to hoping no news was good news with regards to the safety of Stephen and Will. Occasionally I stalked Jude's Facebook page, trying to glean information from his posts: birthday party photos, pictures of family vacations, and videos of the boys' piano recital performances.

As weeks then months went by with no Jude news, my communication with Mark and Tom fell back into the rhythm of occasional emails and phone calls. Mom and I settled back into our life of twice-weekly phone chats plus in-person visits every other weekend. I was always faithful to see my mother every other weekend, so she couldn't say I never visited.

Soon after my mother passed in 2018, all contact stopped between my brothers and me. Mark, the designated executor of Mom's estate, wanted to transfer the duty to me since he and Valerie had moved to Texas; however, Jude and Tom wouldn't allow it. At some point, Mom informed Tom and Jude that Chad had a gambling addiction along with a massive gambling debt. This was laughable, since Chad's part-time job forbid him from gambling or even setting foot inside a casino. I guessed that she told them that during one of her mental crises.

Tom and Jude's anger toward me increased when they learned that Mom left more money to me than them. Planning her estate, she told her financial adviser, "Dina's the only one who takes care of me." In the last four or five years of her life, none of my brothers ever visited Mom, so I could see where she'd think that.

I found Mom's gesture of appreciation a pleasant surprise, deeply touching. My mother expressed with her money what she couldn't say with her words. Mom saw all I did for her. She truly did.

The predicament with my brothers grew so contentious, I told Mark, "While you are settling Mom's estate, I'm going to stop talking to all three of you, because I don't want anything I say to be used against me. If you need anything from me, contact Chad."

In that period of self-imposed silence, I realized things had come full circle. Once again, I felt like an alien within my own family. Somehow Tom and Mark tolerated Jude. Perhaps it was in the name of forgiveness or in hopes that Jude had changed. Or maybe it was simply the distance—over 7,000 nautical miles—that kept their hearts somehow open to him.

Since Jude hadn't unfriended me on social media and I never unfriended him, I saw people I knew leaving their thumbs-up reactions on Jude's posts. Usually it was my sister-in-law, but every now and then, it would be one of my kids. When that happened, I winced. How could they be on both Team Dina and Team Jude?

As I took in Jude's various happy birthday wishes to people and messages of "I'm praying for you!" I snarled. How could Jude believe that God heard his prayers when he abused kids, the least of these? A moment later, I would chastise myself because, really, who can know the heart of God?

Through the years, Jude's friendly guy mask has fooled many

people. He's like a serial killer in the movies, living a secret, evil life.

Years ago, I interviewed a man who had retired from the FBI's crimes against children unit. "Sexual predators are all around you," the child safety expert informed me. "They live next door to you. They serve on boards of directors with you. In church, they sit in the pew beside you."

For the most part, the man said, sexual predators live good and decent lives. There's just one small part of their existence no one knows about, and it's very dark. They adeptly compartmentalize that one small area, believing, "So much of me is good, surely the positive things about me outweigh the one politically incorrect thing."

As he spoke, I pictured Jude clutching a small closed box. Of darkness.

Jude roaming free on the other side of the world is not how I hoped this story would end. Instead I wanted it all tied up with a proverbial bow. In time, though, I recognized that separation from both his family and homeland was Jude's punishment and, to some extent, that felt like enough. His life in sweltering humidity—not to mention extreme traffic, pollution, and political corruption—with a frigid wife, who changed the locks on the house almost weekly in hopes he'd leave forever, sounded like a literal living hell to me. I looked to the horizon, whispering inside my mind, "You sowed misery, Jude, and now you're reaping it."

Then one day in 2023, Jude's location changed. According to Tom, Jude left Leah and the boys and moved to another country alone. Because he could no longer take his family's maltreatment. I wondered what exactly happened to finally shove Jude out of his family's nest. And then in a passing comment, Tom mentioned that one of Jude's boys had begun hitting him. I nodded. I recognized the lashing out of a furious fellow survivor.

The day Jude shared his new location on Facebook—what region in what country—I made note of the information. A few weeks later I filed a report with a child safety organization in that country. To protect the kids there. Because to my mind, Jude can't not do what he does. Sooner or later, he would lift the lid off his box of darkness.

EPILOGUE

Looking back on my life, I recognize it's been an exercise in delayed gratification that has spanned decades. I always knew I'd one day tell my family's secret. I'd be the one to break my family's silence. I was impatient to do so, and yet, it took half of a century to make it happen.

While Chad and I raised our family, I scrawled my story in multiple notebooks. To become a better writer, I read craft books and attended writing conferences. In time I (unsuccessfully) pitched the story idea to agents. Based on their counsel, I started a blog to "build my platform." Determined to improve my craft, I earned an MFA in creative nonfiction.

Still, writing professionals continued to say no to my queries and pitches. One agent even stopped me in the middle of a pitch. "Never use the word *incest* again! No one wants to read about that!"

These days I'm thankful for all the nos. Because not only was my writing not ready back then, the story wasn't over. I pitched my manuscript multiple times before Mom revealed the crime she saw Jude commit against his own child. Once that happened, there was more writing to do.

In addition to writing, for a number of years now, I've worked in the field of child safety. I speak at body safety assemblies in West Virginia public schools, and I blog and speak to adults on the topic as well. I often tell people that working to prevent child sexual abuse is my way of making lemonade from the bitter lemons of my childhood. If telling my story can stop—or better yet, prevent—child sexual abuse, I'm honored to do it.

In the beginning, I identified myself as a survivor of child sexual abuse, sharing that it was both familial and COCSA, or child-on-child sexual abuse. However, it wasn't until 2024 that I added the final detail. My abuse was sibling sexual abuse (SSA). At that point, I felt compelled to be specific about all the details of my abuse because children (and adults) will sometimes disclose if they hear a person speak with the same lived experience as them.

Now that the world has access to my family's story, replete with so many secrets, will they see Jude as the villain? And maybe Mom and Dad as his accomplices, due to their inaction? Perhaps Mark was complicit, too, staying silent for all of his sixty-six years. Am I the heroine of our story, or simply the narrator? I don't know. What do you think?

When Mom told me she witnessed Jude abusing his four-year old son—the boy with the black marble eyes—I yelled inside my mind like I used to. "This all could have been prevented if Mom and Dad had only dealt with Jude's perverted behavior decades ago!"

A serpent-like voice hissed in my ear that day, saying if I'd been more explicit about why Jude visited my room all those nights, maybe someone would've fixed Jude. My silence, then my lack of clarity, allowed the problem to perpetuate.

Thankfully, a still small voice blocked that gut punch, assuring me, "Sweetheart, Little Diane, it was not your fault. You were just a little girl."

All six of us were probably to blame. We all failed. Or maybe a more correct way of saying this is that we all were—probably still are—extremely flawed and very complicated.

And now, only three of us remain: the abuser and his two victims.

My anger has subsided for the most part now. I think much of it was actually rooted in grief. I mourned what should have been. If each of us had done the right things and made the right choices, our lives could have been so different. So much pain might have been avoided. I still want that picture-perfect life. The life of every shiny happy television family.

What grieves me the most is that Jude has never experienced any real consequences for his crimes against our family, against humanity. Not while our parents were alive, and not when they were dead. The six of us never discussed the abuse openly, and no one ever punished Jude.

Until now. Me telling the story of Jude's crimes will be his punishment. This book is his court of law and you, reader, are the jury. Based on the evidence I've presented here, what say you?

As much as I blamed Jude for our family's pandemonium, over time I think I condemned my mother more. For years I made Mom the scapegoat. I heaped all of our family's sins, all of our failures, upon her. At the end of her life, though, I realized Mom was probably not in control of herself during her manic episodes. Maybe during those times, madness took over and poked its pistol into the small of her back and hissed, "Do this. Say that." All my life I believed Mom was simply throwing extreme temper tantrums to get her own way, but perhaps instead of a petulant child being spiteful, she was a grown woman abducted.

As far back as I can remember, my mother's mantra was "I did the best I could." For decades I rejected that hackneyed phrase until finally I grokked that my mother lived three-quarters of her life with the near-constant threat of a hostile takeover. How difficult would it be to run a household, maintain a marriage, and raise a family—sometimes while working full-time—with psychosis lurking in every shadow? You did the best you could, Mom. I see that now. I do. Honestly, your best was not enough, but it was all you had to give.

Once I released Mom from the jail of my own making, it occurred to me I couldn't blame all of our family's struggles on her. Or even Jude. A significant amount of the responsibility belongs to my father. Honestly, I may have known that all along, but if all I ever wanted was to be exactly like him—smart and funny (and yes, emotionally unavailable)—why would I indict him?

In time, I succeeded in becoming my father, the good parts and the bad. It's only been in the last decade that I recognized my emotional reserve as a flaw. For the longest time—and, yes, occasionally even now—Chad had to practically beg me to hold hands, spend time together, or share with him what's on my mind and heart. Slowly, though, I've opened up. Like a peony or a rose.

During one argument a decade ago, I emailed Chad my response, hoping to perfectly articulate my stance, wanting to defuse his tendency to become defensive. "I'd rather have this conversation face-to-face," he typed back, "but if this is all you can manage right now, it's a start."

In recent years, I've worked to become more emotionally healthy. And even though Chad had a head start on me, he's improved in this area as well.

Today, I redistribute our family's sins more fairly. Day-to-day, Dad should have been a more present parent to us kids and a more present husband to Mom. Mom and Dad both should have paid more attention to us kids and parented us more firmly. Mark should have gotten counseling when he melted down at fourteen. When I disclosed what Jude was doing, Mom and Dad should have gotten me help. Tom too. Oh my gracious ... Tom too. When it became clear that Jude had major issues, he should have been removed from the home—to a residential facility or kinship care—to receive the professional help he desperately needed in order to prevent the crimes he went on to commit.

Just as a person can't be helped until they admit they have a problem, a family cannot either. Our parents were ignorant to the fact that a sexual addict (and later, predator) lived among us. They were ignorant to Tom's pain and mine and, to a seemingly lesser extent, Mark's. He hid it well with his golden child behavior.

To further complicate the situation, Dad kept the details of Mom's mental illness from us kids. At some point, Dad should have explained her condition to us so we all could have supported her with more empathy.

Another thing I've reflected on through the years is a misconception I held as a child. For some reason, I always believed every person would experience one and only one significant difficulty during their lifetime. After that—I thought, I hoped—they'd live a life of relative ease. Naively, I thought my childhood experience of sexual abuse would be my only hardship. How wrong I was! Difficult as they were, the discomfort of those childhood nights was eclipsed time and time again. When I committed my mother to a psychiatric ward, twice. As I watched my father lose his beautiful mind to dementia. When Mom told me what she saw transpire between Jude and his son in her guest room.

No one experiences only one hardship. That's not how life works. The tragedies of life break us down, and like a muscle, we respond by growing stronger. If we're lucky. Emotionally speaking, I could probably win a powerlifting competition about now. I desperately want my painful experiences to be over and done with, but I'm not going to be a fool and believe that to be true. As the saying goes, "We can do hard things." I can do hard things.

Now, finally, I've written and published my story. I've fulfilled the promise fourth-grade me made to the world. When I grow up, I'm going to do two things: get counseling and write a book. Mission accomplished, Little Diane. Mission accomplished.

RESOURCES

Websites

5waves.org. The acronym **WAVES** stands for Worldwide, Awareness, Voice, Education, and Support. This website, founded by five women personally impacted by SSA, is devoted to confronting and healing sibling sexual trauma.

siblingstoo.com. This website was created "in order to raise awareness of sibling sexual abuse and its impacts on individuals, families, and society as a whole."

siblingsexualtrauma.com. This is another helpful website with information on the topic of sibling sexual trauma.

incestaware.org. Incest AWARE is an alliance of survivors, supporters, and organizations on a mission to keep children safe from incest through prevention, intervention, recovery, and justice.

d2l.org. The mission of the organization Darkness to Light is to end child sexual abuse. D2L's vision is a world free of child sexual abuse in which adults form prevention-oriented communities. This site features numerous resources, including statistics and training opportunities.

rainn.org. The Rape, Abuse & Incest National Network (RAINN) is the largest anti-sexual violence organization in the

United States. They are committed to helping survivors, educating the public, improving public policy, and offering consulting and training.

1in6.org. At least one in six men have been sexually abused or assaulted. This website exists to support men on their path to a happier, healthier future.

dianetarantini.com. My website features a blog where I write on child safety issues, including sibling sexual abuse.

Books

Sibling Sexual Abuse: A Guide for Confronting America's Silent Epidemic by Brad Watts. This book on the topic of sibling sexual abuse is so valuable, I've read it multiple times.

The Invisible Key: Unlocking the Mystery of My Chronic Pain by Maria Socolof. This memoir tells the story of Socolof's experience with chronic pain and how it was connected to multiple traumas from her life, including an experience of sibling sexual trauma. Survivor note: In my opinion, Socolof's description of her abuse is restrained. But still, if you're easily triggered, be careful.

Resolve: A Story of Courage, Healthy Inquiry and Recovery from Sibling Sexual Abuse by Alice Perle. Perle's memoir *Resolve* tells the story of her experience with sibling sexual abuse. Interspersed throughout the story is research on the topic. Survivor note: In my opinion, the description of the abuse is graphic. If you're easily triggered, be careful with this one.

The Body Keeps the Score: Brain, Mind, and Body in the Healing of Trauma by Bessel van der Kolk. Recommended by so many child safety experts, this book helped me see that a number of issues I live with are due to my childhood trauma.

Boundaries: When to Say Yes, How to Say No to Take Control of Your Life by Henry Cloud and John Townsend. This is one of the most helpful books I've ever read. The principles outlined in this book are useful for every relationship, in my opinion.

Mothers Who Can't Love: A Healing Guide for Daughters by Susan Forward, PhD. When my mother was being especially difficult, I found this book very helpful.

Will I Ever Be Good Enough? Healing the Daughters of Narcissistic Mothers by Karyl McBride, PhD. This book was also helpful in navigating my difficult relationship with my mother.

Programs

iamonevoice.org/unleash. The UNLEASH program—created by Nicole Braddock Bromley—is an eight-week virtual support group for survivors of sexual abuse. Bromley, a survivor and survivor's advocate, facilitates the sessions along with a trauma-informed therapist. Having participated in UNLEASH two times, I highly recommend it as a prelude or addition to therapeutic counseling.

helpwantedprevention.org. This website is an online course to provide help to people attracted to younger children. It was created to give tools to support individuals in their effort to live a safe, healthy, nonoffending life.

ABOUT THE AUTHOR

Diane Tarantini is a dynamic communicator who speaks and writes primarily on the topic of child safety. As a survivor of child sexual abuse, a body safety educator in the state of West Virginia, and an author, blogger, and journalist focused on child safety, Tarantini researches the topic to know what threats to kids are trending and how to deal with them. She then distills the information and delivers it to both adults and children: in person and on her website, diane-tarantini.com.

Tarantini lives in a 114-year-old Sears kit house in Almost Heaven, West Virginia, with her husband, Tony, and their two cats, Bonnie Agnes and Boots Louise. Grown and flown, but living not too far away, are their three awesome children.

For more information, visit: www.dianetarantini.com
Or email Tarantini at: diane@dianetarantini.com

You can also follow Tarantini at:

facebook.com/DianeTarantiniAuthor

instagram.com/writingdianet
tiktok.com/@dianetarantiniauthor
pinterest.com/dianetarantiniauthor

To hear from Tarantini on a regular basis, sign up for her monthly e-newsletter at dianetarantini.com.

WHAT YOU SHOULD DO NOW...

Write a review on Amazon.com. After you've finished *Everyone Was Silent*, please consider writing a review for the book on Amazon.com. Reviews are the #1 way you can help a writer get found in the vast ocean of 32 million books that are listed on the site. When a book receives a significant number of positive reviews, Amazon notices and "pushes" the book to shoppers they think may like it. You can help make that happen!

Write a review on Goodreads.com. Goodreads is a site for book lovers. If you mention that you're reading *Everyone Was Silent* or review it afterward, it will help the book's "discoverability" factor.

Tell your friends about *Everyone Was Silent*. Word-of-mouth advertising is one of the best things that can happen for a book. If you found value in reading *Everyone Was Silent*, recommend it to your friends who love books. Especially if they love memoirs. Or, if you know they've experienced one of the issues discussed in the book.

Post a photo of your copy of *Everyone Was Silent* on your social media platforms. This will build "buzz" for the book and may lead to sales! Please include #EveryoneWasSilent on your posts so I can use it on my social media!

Ask your local library to carry *Everyone Was Silent.* As a card-carrying member, you have clout at your public library. Librarians listen to their patrons.

THE BRAVE KNIGHT

Mere months before The Great Pause shut down the world, Diane Tarantini was asked by a child safety expert to write a book to show children, in a nonthreatening way, the concept of grooming, the process by which a sexual predator gains the trust of a potential victim and sometimes their family members.

The Brave Knight is that book.

- **The nonprofit Libera purchased 7,000 copies *of The Brave Knight*, one for every foster child in West Virginia.**
- **The West Virginia Library Commission chose *The Brave Knight* to be the 2023 "Summer Read" in every public library in the state.**

"In *The Brave Knight*, Tarantini articulates incredibly complex child abuse grooming techniques/dynamics (i.e., desensitizing physical contact, isolation from familial supports, love for perpetrators, disparity of social power), and somehow does it in an age-appropriate, nonthreatening way. A brilliant, compelling, and inspiring resource for kids and those who love them."

—**Robert Peters**, Director of Institutional Response at G.R.A.C.E., founder of Shield Task Force, former prosecuting attorney, former US Marine

"This book should be in every elementary school in the United States and in the hands of every adult engaged in the health and welfare of young people. It is not only an essential resource for empowering and equipping children but a valuable resource in identifying at-risk and victimized children."

—**Gregory D Cooper**, APRN-BC, Psychiatric Nurse Practitioner

"This book is a wonderful tool to spark some important conversations. My 4-year-old was such a fan that she asked for it to be read three times, one by each adult in the house so that everyone would know about safety. She thought the most important lesson is that a kid can always tell their mom when someone makes them feel not safe.

On a professional note, I have worked in the child safety field for over 20 years and am always so excited when good quality materials become available for kids. This book is obviously a labor of love. It does a good job of starting quality conversations that aren't rooted in fear, but instead are centered in empowerment."

—**Alison Feigh**, Director of the Jacob Wetterling Resource Center at Zero Abuse Project

"As a professional who works in the field of child advocacy, I would definitely recommend this book for any child in your life. Childhood sexual abuse and grooming aren't topics that people talk about regularly, and they can be uncomfortable. Diane does a great job addressing abuse in a way children can understand. *The Brave Knight* is a great tool for starting those conversations and an invaluable resource for children and families!"

—**Stacy Deel**, Director of Operations and Communications at West Virginia Child Advocacy Network

The Brave Knight is available at dianetaranti.com and amazon.com.

NOTES

35. HYPERSEXUALITY

1. Sara Solovitch, "Opening the Door on Hypersexuality," bphope: Hope and Harmony for People With Bipolar, last modified July 28, 2021, http://www.bphope.com/opening-the-door-on-hypersexuality.
2. Kelly Connell and Valencia Higuera, "Bipolar Disorder and Sexual Health, Healthline, last modified on February 12, 2021, https://www.healthline.com/health/bipolar-disorder/sexual-health.
3. Idem.
4. These statistics come from research by Barbara Geller, MD, professor of psychiatry at the Washington University in St. Louis. Sara Solovitch, "Opening the Door on Hypersexuality," bphope: Hope and Harmony for People With Bipolar, last modified July 28, 2021, http://www.bphope.com/opening-the-door-on-hypersexuality.
5. Demitri Papolos, "Straight Talk about Hypersexuality in Children with Bipolar," bphope: Hope and Harmony for People With Bipolar, last modified March 13, 2023, https://www.bphope.com/kids-children-teens/straight-talk-about-kids-and-hypersexuality.

43. RESEARCH

1. "Pessimism About Pedophilia," *Harvard Health Letter* 27, no. 1 (July 2010): 1–3.
2. "Sexual Assault," RAINN (Rape, Abuse & Incest National Network), https://www.rainn.org/articles/sexual-assault.
3. David Goldberg, "I, Pedophile," *The Atlantic*, August 26, 2013, https://www.theatlantic.com/health/archive/2013/08/i-pedophile/278921.
4. Alice Dreger, "What Can Be Done About Pedophilia?" *The Atlantic*, August 26, 2013, https://www.theatlantic.com/health/archive/2013/08/what-can-be-done-about-pedophilia/279024.
5. Mark Williams, "Father-Son Incest: A Review and Analysis of Reported Incidents," *Clinical Social Work Journal* 16, no. 2 (June 1988): 165–179.

Made in the USA
Columbia, SC
20 July 2024